No Longer an ORPHAN

NEVER ABANDONED, NEVER ALONE

Dana Stone

WestBow Press
A DIVISION OF THOMAS NELSON
& ZONDERVAN

Copyright © 2015 Dana Stone.

Author photo: Cory Hale
Family 2015: Kimberly Dendy
Netanya 2015: Johan Etsebeth

All rights reserved. No part of this book may be used or reproduced by any means, graphic, electronic, or mechanical, including photocopying, recording, taping or by any information storage retrieval system without the written permission of the publisher except in the case of brief quotations embodied in critical articles and reviews.

Scripture taken from the Holy Bible, NEW INTERNATIONAL VERSION®. Copyright © 1973, 1978, 1984 by Biblica, Inc. All rights reserved worldwide. Used by permission. NEW INTERNATIONAL VERSION® and NIV® are registered trademarks of Biblica, Inc. Use of either trademark for the offering of goods or services requires the prior written consent of Biblica US, Inc.

This book is a work of non-fiction. Unless otherwise noted, the author and the publisher make no explicit guarantees as to the accuracy of the information contained in this book and in some cases, names of people and places have been altered to protect their privacy.

WestBow Press books may be ordered through booksellers or by contacting:

WestBow Press
A Division of Thomas Nelson & Zondervan
1663 Liberty Drive
Bloomington, IN 47403
www.westbowpress.com
1 (866) 928-1240

Because of the dynamic nature of the Internet, any web addresses or links contained in this book may have changed since publication and may no longer be valid. The views expressed in this work are solely those of the author and do not necessarily reflect the views of the publisher, and the publisher hereby disclaims any responsibility for them.

Any people depicted in stock imagery provided by Thinkstock are models, and such images are being used for illustrative purposes only. Certain stock imagery © Thinkstock.

ISBN: 978-1-5127-0541-6 (sc)
ISBN: 978-1-5127-0543-0 (hc)
ISBN: 978-1-5127-0542-3 (e)

Library of Congress Control Number: 2015912153

Print information available on the last page.

WestBow Press rev. date: 07/31/2015

Contents

Chapter 1	The God Who Creates Us	1
Chapter 2	The God Who Is Right on Time	9
Chapter 3	The God Who Knows Us	14
Chapter 4	The God Who Prepares Us	21
Chapter 5	The God Who Orders All Things	25
Chapter 6	The God Who Sings over Us	30
Chapter 7	The God Who Calls Us by Name	35
Chapter 8	The God Who Battles for Us	41
Chapter 9	The God Who Gives Us Peace	47
Chapter 10	The God Who Watches over Us	52
Chapter 11	The God Who Provides for Us	56
Chapter 12	The God Who We Can Trust	62
Chapter 13	The God Who Gives Us Rest	68
Chapter 14	The God Who Brings Exceeding Joy	71
Chapter 15	The God Who Hears Our Prayers	77
Chapter 16	The God Who Is Faithful	83
Chapter 17	The God Who Never Leaves Us	90
Chapter 18	The God Who Completes Us	96
Chapter 19	The God Who Ordains Our Days	101
Chapter 20	The God Who Heals Our Heart	107
Chapter 21	The God Who Comforts Us	115
Chapter 22	The God Who Is True to His Word	122
Chapter 23	The God Who Is Father to the Fatherless	126
Chapter 24	The God Who Loves Us Unconditionally	131
Chapter 25	The God Who Sees Us	137
Chapter 26	The God Who Deserves Our Praise	142
Chapter 27	The God Who Calls Us His Own	145

Dedication

To Todd, Joshua, Jacob, Netanya, Noah, Tabitha, Skyler, Ava and Emma. There is no greater honor to me than bearing the name wife, mother and grandmother. I am blessed beyond measure to share this wonderful thing called life with each of you. I love you today, tomorrow and always.

FOREWORD

Have you ever struggled to feel valued, accepted or loved? Maybe you've known what it is to be betrayed or abandoned. Maybe you simply have felt alone and isolated. All of us find ourselves in seasons and moments where we long to be loved and accepted, valued for who we are. We thirst to be a part of something more significant, something bigger than ourselves and greater than what we can accomplish alone. We wonder if our lives matter and if there is a bigger purpose in all the pain. Wounds, lies or even subtle comparisons have caused us to draw conclusions about ourselves (and others) that are simply off-point and in many cases a flat out lie.

God never intended for any of us to go it alone. He purposefully brings people into our lives who can teach us to draw closer to Him. God is constantly at work adjusting our vision to align with His own and using the insights and lessons He's taught others to help us along the way.

This is where Dana Stone has often intersected the lives of so many people, including my own. She has helped many overcome pain by introducing them to her best friend, Jesus Christ, and revealing His heart to rescue, restore and even adopt each of us. The first time I met Dana I knew immediately that she was special. She had an uncanny ability to put others at ease and a servant heart that practically glowed with love. She made others feel seen, heard and understood. She quietly went about the business of investing in the ministry of Gateway women, always making herself available for a divine encounter or a spontaneous moment of encouragement.

Over the years of our friendship, I've had a front row seat to watch countless men and women quietly draw near, sit down at her knee and wait to receive encouragement, counsel and even revelation. We have often laughed and said that there must be a "people magnet" in her desk side chair. Throughout the day people appear, sit for a moment with this sage, and then arise to go on their way. Each one comes for something different. Some need reassurance, some to find salvation, some to have their gifts revealed and some to overcome feelings of rejection, isolation or loss.

When you hold **No Longer an Orphan: Never Abandoned, Never Alone** in your hand, it is as if you are pulling up a chair at Dana's knee. This is not just another "feel good" read or "how to" book. Dana's been through some stuff. You will relate to her. She's authentic, trust worthy and transparent. Each chapter will take you along on the journey of Dana's spiritual growth and the story of her beautiful daughter Netanya's miraculous rescue and adoption.

With careful attention, Dana will reach into the depths of her love walk with Christ and pull out the perfect pearl or two of God's love that will speak to you. As you move through each chapter, Dana will reveal another dimension of His love and character. As you discover the beauty of His personality, experience the fruit of His love and begin to walk in His gifts, you will come to terms with who you are, how you are fashioned and what makes you unique and special. As they take root in the depths of your own love walk with Christ, you will be healed.

I encourage you to pull up a chair and open your heart to whatever the Holy Spirit wants to teach you through Dana's life. I pray that your own story of rescue, redemption and adoption will unfold before your very eyes and that as you read, the Holy Spirit will show you places in your heart that need His truth, His touch and His love. I believe you will be challenged, inspired and led to a greater understanding of the multi-faceted heart of God toward you. When you know Him more fully, then you will see yourself through His eyes. His eyes never lie. You will know that you are never abandoned, never alone.

Jan Greenwood
Pastor of Gateway Women, Gateway Church
Author of *Women at War*

Psalm 139:1-11

"You have searched me, Lord, and You know me.
You know when I sit and when I rise; You
perceive my thoughts from afar.
You discern my going out and my lying down;
You are familiar with all my ways.
Before a word is on my tongue, You, Lord, know it completely.
You hem me in behind and before, and
You lay your hand upon me.
Such knowledge is too wonderful for
me, too lofty for me to attain.
Where can I go from Your Spirit? Where
can I flee from Your presence?
If I go up to the heavens, You are there; if I make
my bed in the depths, You are there.
If I rise on the wings of the dawn, if I
settle on the far side of the sea,
even there Your hand will guide me, Your
right hand will hold me fast.
If I say, "Surely the darkness will hide me and
the light become night around me,"
even the darkness will not be dark to You;
the night will shine like the day,
for darkness is as light to You.
For You created my inmost being; You knit
me together in my mother's womb.
I praise You because I am fearfully and wonderfully made;
Your works are wonderful and I know that full well."

The God Who Creates Us

Psalm 139:13-14

For You formed my inward parts; You knitted me together in my mother's womb. I praise You, for I am fearfully and wonderfully made. Wonderful are Your works; my soul knows it very well.

Chapter 1

You did what? rolled through my head as I tried not to shout it out loud. My husband Todd had just walked in from work and casually announced, "I called the Gladney Center today to order a packet on international adoption. It's time to go get our daughter. What do you think about that?"

I had waited for this moment for so long, and now that it was finally happening I almost couldn't believe it. Trying to curb my excitement for fear he might change his mind, I cautiously asked, "Oh, really? What made you do that?"

What a silly question! I knew exactly who, not what, had caused this 180-degree change in my husband. I stood there looking at him; amazed at the gift God had given me eleven years earlier. Here was a man that knew me better than anyone else. He knew exactly who I was, and he loved me unconditionally. As my heart burst with joy and appreciation I couldn't believe what a miracle it was to have him in my life.

Dana Stone

Todd and I met at Texas A&M in the fall of 1981. At that time I was a totally broken person. Although I had been raised in a pretty typical home I always felt alone in the world. My father was an army man, and we moved often during my childhood. I never had the chance to really take root and establish lasting friendships. I lived in a tightly structured home with little outward demonstration of love or affection. Responsibility, order and respect were the values that permeated everything we did and said. As children of an officer, my brother, sister and I were raised to be seen and not heard. As the youngest child, I spent a lot of time alone playing in my room or reading.

My dad's military career was his life. The men he commanded and served alongside were his family. He was gone more than he was home for much of my early years, and when he *was* home there seemed to be an invisible wall that made any type of emotional connection between him and us very difficult. He never quite understood how to invest himself into the lives of his children.

My mom had her hands full trying to raise three children on her own most of the time. The responsibilities that went with being an officer's wife kept her very busy and left little time for anything besides the basics when it came to family life. My parents were kind people and did the best they could, but nurturing was not their strong suit. I knew they cared about me, but I never felt of much value to anyone. I tried for years to gain my father's love and approval but was never able to get past that invisible wall that separated him from the rest of our family.

When I was fifteen, we moved from California to San Antonio, Texas. Daddy had been assigned to Ft. Sam Houston, and for the first time in my life we were going to live off post in our very own home. We arrived in San Antonio on my fifteenth birthday, and I started high school the next week. I felt terribly shy and insecure, especially since once again I would have to find my place and make new friends. I knew first appearances were important, so I made sure that my outfit for the first day of school was perfect.

I got on the bus that day wearing my California inspired mini skirt, only to quickly discover that in Texas *midi* skirts were the latest fashion statement. I stuck out like a sore thumb those first two weeks until Mom could find the time to get me some new clothes. It was definitely not the way I hoped to begin my high school years!

Daddy ended up retiring from the army the next year, and that decision allowed me to attend the same school all four years. I found a group of friends, got involved in a few school organizations and for the most part, had a normal high school experience. What most people didn't know was that I still felt alone. Even in the midst of thousands of screaming fans at a typical Friday night football game in Texas, I felt invisible. I wanted so badly to know I belonged and to feel seen and heard. It just never seemed to happen.

I was accepted to Texas A&M my senior year. I was excited to be following in the footsteps of my older brother and sister and become a Texas Aggie. I hoped this would allow me to finally find my place in the world. That summer I started dating my very first boyfriend. I always went to dances with guy friends in high school but never had an actual boyfriend, so to have one now was pretty exciting. For the first time in my life I felt like I mattered to someone. And the fact that he was a year older than me and already in college made me feel even more special.

He was a nice enough guy and we had fun together, but my longing to feel loved and valued by him was violently shattered one weekend during a camping trip. The trauma of what he did to me left me broken physically, mentally and emotionally. I lost all sense of who I was. I was so ashamed of what had happened that I never told anyone. I didn't seek out help or counseling and without that critical support, a piece of me died inside. I cried myself to sleep almost every night for months, but put a smile on my face for the outside world. I decided that somehow I must have deserved what had happened to me and even continued dating him for several more months. In an attempt to make sense of what happened, I made a tragic decision to believe the lie that my role in life was to be seen and not heard. I determined that the only way I would ever receive the love and acceptance I so desperately sought was to have no voice at all.

So I arrived at college as a young woman seeking love and acceptance in all the wrong ways. I made so many poor choices that first year of college trying to fill the empty places in my heart where love longed to take hold. And then I met him.

From our very first date, I could tell Todd was different. He knew who I was, and he knew all about the choices I was making; yet he saw past it all. He saw things in me that I didn't even know existed. He saw strength and wisdom. He saw purpose and passion. He saw an amazing testimony just waiting to be shared. And he spoke life into all that he saw. He reminded me on a daily basis that I was a young woman who deserved and should expect men to honor and respect me, and above all else I deserved someone who would guard my heart. Over the next two and a half years, he showed me what that kind of love looked like. Todd quietly mirrored the character of God and filled the holes in my heart with truth, love and commitment. He guarded my heart with great care, and he loved me unconditionally. I began to see myself through his eyes, and through those eyes I saw Jesus for the first time. For the first time in my life I didn't feel alone.

Todd and I married in 1984. We had just graduated from college and had wonderful visions of career, travel and fun adventures. He started working as a general contractor, and I began my career as an elementary school teacher. We spent most of our first year and a half of marriage digging into our careers, making new friends and traveling. When we decided to start a family, I discovered that there was a significant problem; I could not get pregnant. We tried unsuccessfully for about eighteen months before we consulted a fertility doctor.

It was December and we were planning to accompany my parents and sister to Germany for Christmas to visit my brother and his family who were stationed there in the army. I had an appointment that day to begin testing in hopes of finding the underlying cause of my infertility. I was excited when I arrived at the doctor's office, but also a little nervous.

The nurse did some routine tests and left the room. When my doctor came back in he looked very serious. He closed the door and sat down next to me. "Dana", he said quietly. "You are going to have a very difficult time getting pregnant through fertility treatments." My heart sank. I started thinking about how I was going to break the news to Todd and how I was going to tell family members who were anxiously awaiting the results of this appointment. Tears began to well up in my eyes and I looked at him for some kind of understanding. What I saw instead when I looked up was my doctor grinning at me… and then he said six words that literally rocked my world. "Because, my dear, you already are."

If you have ever watched a Charlie Brown cartoon, you can visualize what happened next, because I looked like Snoopy doing his happy dance! My doctor estimated that I was about nine weeks into my pregnancy, and after an initial exam he told me, "When you get back from Germany, we'll do a sonogram. Just relax, enjoy the trip, and have fun while you're there."

I headed straight to Todd's office. He was expecting me after my appointment and I knew he would be anxious to hear about the process we would undergo. I closed his door and repeated the doctor's words to him. He just sat there without moving for a minute or two. Then with big tears in his eyes he finally muttered a profound, "Huh?"

After I told him all that had happened at the doctor's office he began to grasp the fact that I was indeed pregnant. We spent the next hour calling family members to share the exciting news. Pregnant! We were going to have a baby! It was wonderful news and we thought the timing was perfect. Christmas with all my family then we would start the New Year with a baby on the way. What could be better? That night we went out and celebrated the start of our new family.

As a prelude to our trip to Germany we flew to San Antonio two days before Christmas to spend the night with my family before flying out the next morning. We couldn't wait to celebrate Christmas together. We helped my parents finish packing and spent the evening looking at maps and event itineraries. The excitement was electrifying. We all said goodnight and headed to our rooms for the night.

Late that night, I started to bleed heavily. My mother, who was a nurse, was there to help. "Dana, there's not much we can do", she said. She sounded so sad as she sat by the side of my bed and tried to comfort me. After she left Todd and I lay in bed holding each other and cried. Old feelings of being alone came flooding back. Thankfully Todd had been raised in a Christian home that believed in the power of prayer, and he knew who to call out to in our time of need. He knew we *weren't* alone. He placed his hands gently on my stomach and prayed Ezekiel 6:6 over our baby,

> Then I passed by and saw you kicking about in your blood, and as you lay there in your blood I said to you, Live!

With all our hearts we believed that God would speak life into our unborn child that night. We clung to that Scripture through one of the longest nights of our lives. By the next morning, the bleeding had increased and we knew it was time to go to the hospital for help. Todd rushed me to the emergency room of a local hospital. They took some brief information and prepared me for the worst, but when the doctor did a sonogram, he was stunned. God had shown up in a miraculous way.

Our baby was still there, heartbeat and all! After a few more tests, the doctor determined that our baby was not in immediate danger. He also told us that Germany was out of the question and that I needed several days of bed rest with minimal movement. He reminded us that we were not out of the woods, and that the next week was critical. A decision had to be made quickly because our plane was scheduled to leave within the next two hours. No one in our family wanted to leave, but after much discussion, we finally decided that mom and dad would go ahead with their trip to Germany and my sister would stay in San Antonio with us. It was difficult for my parents to leave, but they knew my brother would be disappointed if no one came.

My sister was my rock during the next few days. She took us to her house and put me straight to bed, and then she put her plan to save Christmas for us in action! Because we were planning to be in Germany for Christmas there was no tree, no decorations and no gifts. Todd and my sister headed to the store to get food for our Christmas meal and to the mall to try to find some decorations and gifts. By the time they got back, they were brimming with Christmas spirit and it quickly spread throughout the house. We had a wonderful time together, and my sister made the most scrumptious Cornish hens for our Christmas Day feast. After several more days of rest, Todd got me on a plane, and he started home in the car.

We went to the hospital the next day for a follow up sonogram and received wonderful news. Our baby was perfectly healthy and growing. We discovered through the sonogram that I was really only four weeks pregnant. Pregnancy tests weren't as sophisticated back then, so our doctor was surprised at how early my pregnancy had been detected. Todd and I knew in our hearts that God had been watching over us and that it was His hand of protection and healing that had kept our baby safe. In that moment, I was reminded that God values and cherishes all of His children. He created each of us with love and care and He had a wonderful and marvelous plan for *every* life. This little baby growing inside of me was our miracle baby; we just didn't know we would have three more.

God, your Word says that You created me with great care. There is no one else like me. I am fearfully and wonderfully made. You see me. I am loved, accepted and cherished by You. I choose to see the value and importance my life holds. When I feel alone I will call out to You and receive Your unconditional love and grace. I am not alone.

THE GOD WHO IS RIGHT ON TIME

Ecclesiastes 3:1

To everything there is a season, and a time for every matter or purpose under heaven.

CHAPTER 2

August 16 After sixteen hours of hard labor, my doctor finally decided I was not going to be able to have a traditional delivery. So at 7:25 p.m., Joshua Gordon Stone was born by Caesarean section weighing in at nine pounds one ounce, and twenty-two inches long.

Todd was the first person to hold our son. As he walked Joshua down to the nursery he prayed over him thanking the Lord for the miracle that He had given us; a beautiful, perfectly healthy son. It was an incredible experience, as all parents know, to be blessed with such an amazing gift. We were in awe and totally head over heels in love. We looked forward to the days ahead as a family of three. But God had just begun to unfold His plan for children in our lives.

When Joshua was two years old I found out I was pregnant again. Our doctor did a sonogram and told us I was about eleven weeks pregnant. We watched in amazement as we saw this tiny baby with a strong heartbeat on the screen. We were thrilled that another sweet child was on the way! The next day we celebrated our fifth wedding anniversary with great excitement and anticipation.

Two days later, I woke up bleeding again and found myself back in the emergency room. This time the news was not good. Our precious baby had died. Within minutes, I was being wheeled into the operating room for surgery. It was a crushing blow for us, and we grieved the loss of our child. It was a very difficult, sad and lonely time for both of us, yet God made Himself so real to us through His Word and through many good friends. On days when sadness enveloped my heart it never failed that I would receive a call, a sweet note in the mail, flowers would be delivered or a meal would appear at our front door. We learned a lot during the days and months to follow about trusting God's plan for our lives and resting in the peace that He alone could provide. We learned the value and importance of community, and the people that God used to bring healing and comfort to our broken hearts daily amazed us. We learned we weren't alone.

As our hearts continued to heal we focused on our family and our daily lives. Todd was now working as a general contractor for a company based out of Ohio. In May of 1990, he was abruptly given twenty-four hours notice that the office was shutting down. Todd quickly began to close up the office, take care of clients and reassure his wife that everything would be just fine. He knew that God would continue to provide for our family. His quiet assurance and strong belief calmed my nerves and eased my concerns.

That evening as I showered I found a lump in my right breast. It concerned me because the lump was hard and very defined. I immediately told Todd and because his company's medical insurance was going to lapse at midnight the following day, we decided to schedule an appointment with my doctor as quickly as possible.

In the morning I checked again and the lump was still there. I called my doctor and once he understood our circumstances he agreed to see me that day. His nurse performed the routine tests they always run and left the exam room. As I waited for the doctor, I checked for the lump again, but this time it was gone! All this panic and concern and now it is gone? I was prepared to be very embarrassed and apologetic!

The door opened and in walked my doctor. He came in with a smile on his face but said nothing. He examined me, and I could tell he wasn't finding a lump either. Embarrassed, I laid there silently wanting to crawl under a rock.

Finally, he sat down and said, "Dana, I want to assure you that I didn't detect a lump in your breast, but I *can* tell you that I *did* detect something else that will give you a pretty big lump in your tummy over the next nine months. Congratulations, you are pregnant!"

I lay there for a few seconds thinking to myself, *I didn't just hear that. I could not have just heard that. I think I DID just hear that.* I sat up and he was grinning from ear to ear. A sonogram confirmed that I was indeed six weeks pregnant. This time everything looked great. I drove home feeling a major case of deja vu.

Todd was home when I arrived and once again I sat him down to explain the results of the doctor's findings. He wasn't expecting what I said next: "Well, honey, do you know where we can find some good maternity insurance really fast?" After he recovered from the shock he jumped into action and spent the rest of the day on the phone trying to extend our insurance coverage.

Once again God's timing was perfect and He provided for our every need. We had no job and a baby on the way, but the hand of our loving God covered us. Over the next few months, friends gathered together and surprised us with bags of food, clothes for Joshua, money for bills and even a few new maternity outfits for me! They had a baby shower for us and provided for every need that came up. During a time that we could have once again felt alone, God showed us in so many tangible ways that He was right by our side.

This pregnancy progressed very normally and without any problems until the actual day we were set to deliver. Due to the difficulties I had with Joshua's birth, our doctor had prearranged a Caesarean section for January 23. We woke up early that morning full of excitement and anticipation. Leaving a sleeping three and a half year old with a good friend, we headed to the hospital. We checked in at 5:00 a.m. and were told that we would go into surgery in less than an hour.

At 5:30 a.m., our anesthesiologist came in, prepared me for surgery and gave me an epidural. Then we waited for my doctor... and waited... and waited. Finally, the nurse came in and told us that another patient had come in very close to delivery. My doctor had decided to deliver that baby first and then come in to deliver ours. Unfortunately, no one had told the anesthesiologist. He was rather irritated because, by that time, my epidural was beginning to wear off and he had to administer more of the medicine. I began to labor in my breathing, and I remember that I felt like I was forgetting how to breathe.

Another issue the medical staff was dealing with during that time was that our baby was so big that he was pressing on a major artery. Every time they tried to lay me on my back I would pass out, my pulse would drop dramatically, and I would stop breathing. This happened four or five times in a row, and the team was having a difficult time trying to stabilize me. The doctor was rushed to the operating room and quickly assessed the situation. I was pretty incoherent and very nauseated so the decision was made to have Todd leave the room as they tried to work on me. They turned me on my side and began furiously trying to stabilize my blood pressure and heart rate. After about fifteen minutes, they were comfortable enough to allow Todd back in to be with me, and within a few minutes, Jacob Glover Stone was born. He was even bigger than his brother had been, weighing in at nine pounds eleven ounces and was twenty-two and a half inches long. And boy did he come out screaming!

As he had with Joshua, Todd was the first person to hold our son. As he whisked Jacob off to the nursery, he quietly prayed over him and thanked the Lord for protecting our son. So God had given us our second miracle baby. Two beautiful sons, what more could we ask for?

A conversation near the end of my second pregnancy still plays vividly in my mind. Todd and I were in the doctor's office meeting with him about the upcoming C-section. He was asking us a lot of basic questions, and then he asked us one that neither one of us had even given a moment's thought. His question was a simple one, "Would you like to have your tubes tied while we are in there? A lot of people do after two children. It won't be any problem and it is a very simple procedure."

Todd and I just looked at each other. At that time it sounded reasonable. Our initial response was a probable yes, but then God did what only He can do; He spoke to my heart. He planted the seed in my spirit that would take years to come to fruition. His question was a simple one, *Do you trust me?* I didn't say anything in the office, but later that day I told Todd what I had heard, and that I wasn't ready to make such a big decision. Todd's response was simple and sweet, "That's fine, whatever you want Babe. We can always trust His plan for our lives."

I am so thankful the Lord chose to impart His perfect timing into our lives that day. He had begun to change my heart about more children. It would take six years to change Todd's.

―∞―

God, your Word says that there is a time and purpose for everything in our lives. When life seems to not make sense, when I struggle with understanding your plan for my life, I choose to look to you and trust that your timing is always perfect and that your plans will not be delayed. I am not alone.

The God Who Knows Us

John 10:14

I am the Good Shepherd- I know my sheep and my sheep know me.

CHAPTER 3

Over the next few years, we settled into family life with two wonderful, healthy sons. Joshua and Jacob were a delight. Our days were filled with the usual ups and downs of parenting, but we were enjoying every moment.

As we grew closer together as a family, I was also growing in my faith. We became involved at our church, and through the community of believers there, I was beginning to grow in my spiritual walk. Todd had given his life to the Lord when he was ten, and had been raised in a home that welcomed the Holy Spirit into their daily lives. Although I believed in God, I had never been taught about who Jesus was and what He had done for me. It wasn't until a letter arrived in the mail one day that I truly began to understand the need for Jesus in my own life.

It was the fall of 1991, and I grabbed the mail from the mailbox that afternoon. I threw it on the counter and rushed to fix dinner. After the kids were in bed, I picked up the mail and saw a letter addressed to me in Daddy's handwriting. This was really unusual because he wasn't much of a letter writer. I sat down and opened the envelope. Inside I found two typewritten pages and as I began to read the letter from Daddy, my heart began to break in a million pieces. The letter was very formal, no frills--just facts. He wrote that the same letter had been sent to my brother and sister. His words were calculated and firm with no room for interpretation; after thirty-nine years of marriage, he had decided to leave my mom. He listed many reasons why he had come to this decision, and let me know that there was no room for discussion or compromise. At the end of the letter he asked me not to call my mom because he planned to tell her the next night.

I remember slipping out of the chair onto the floor in total disbelief. My mind couldn't comprehend the words and actions of my own father. In that moment, I felt like a little girl again; totally abandoned. Here I was, a thirty year old married woman with two children and yet the little girl inside me, the one who had spent so much of her growing up years desperately trying to gain the attention and affection of her earthly father, lay on the floor paralyzed by an overwhelming sense of grief and sadness. I wanted to call my mom, but I knew there was no way I could stop the pain from coming.

The next few weeks were some of the most difficult days of my life. After Daddy told Mom, he immediately moved out. I drove down to be with her and try to comfort her as best I could. While I was there, Dad called and asked to meet with me. The meeting did not go well, and his words crushed my spirit. When I drove home a few days later, I cried out to God and begged Him to take the pain, anger, hurt and disappointment away. The silence inside the car and inside my heart was deafening. It was in that silence that I finally realized that I needed HIM. I needed to know this Jesus that I was learning more and more about every day.

I called a good friend of mine and asked her if we could meet. I knew she would be able to answer all my questions without making me feel embarrassed or ashamed. We spent the next eight hours talking. She answered every question I had with ease and grace. She didn't rush me and she shared her heart--HIS heart--with me so tenderly. At the end she finally looked at me and said four words that would change my life forever:

"Are you ready yet?"

And I was. My heart and my mind finally understood that God knew everything about me. He knew all the good and all the bad. He knew me better than anyone else ever could, because He created me. And I knew that He loved me just the way I was.

So on September 23, 1991, in a quiet corner of her parent's home, my friend led me in a simple prayer, and I gave my life to the Lord. I asked Jesus to come into my heart. I thanked Him for dying on the cross for me and I gave Him permission to be the Lord of my life. And in that moment, the old Dana died and I became a new person in Christ. I knew I would never be alone again. I knew that from this moment on, I had a Father who would never leave me. This Father would love me unconditionally because I mattered to Him. He saw me. I was now HIS child. I would never have to feel alone again.

From that day forward, my walk with the Lord took on a whole new dimension. Scripture began to come alive. I would read passages I had read countless times before and suddenly they would make sense. The words brought new life, joy and an overwhelming sense of peace into every area of my life. Each time feelings of hurt, anger or sadness would rise up in me, the Lord would bring peace and restoration. He would show me through His Word how to handle each and every situation that I encountered. It was during that time God showed me the plan He had for my relationship with Daddy. I was reading in Ezra one morning and Chapter 9:8-9 said,

> But now, for a brief moment, the Lord our God has been gracious in leaving us a remnant and giving us a firm place in his sanctuary, and so our God gives light to our eyes and a little relief in our bondage. Though we are slaves, our God has not deserted us in our bondage. He has shown us

> kindness in the sight of the Kings of Persia. He has granted us new life to rebuild the house of our God and repair its ruins and He has given us a wall of protection in Judah and Jerusalem.

In that moment He broke my heart for Daddy. I knew that God was calling ME to be that wall of protection, that remnant. I knew that God was somehow going to bring life out of death and repair to the ruins that were our family. I also knew that it was going to require laying everything down, my hurt, my anger and my disappointment. My assignment was to bring light, relief and kindness into places that were filled with darkness and despair. I had no idea at that time just how long that assignment would last, but I knew that I wouldn't have to do it alone.

It was a sweet time of leaning on Jesus and trusting that He would help me each step of the way. I looked forward to each day, excited to see what the Lord would show me. Life continued to bring its challenges but I knew I didn't have to do it alone. I knew I had a heavenly Father who was right by my side all the time.

Todd and I grew so much closer over the next several years because we were finally able to connect on a spiritual level. We enjoyed praying together as a couple, we studied the Word together and we started leading a Bible study in our home. It was a joy to be able to share the power and peace of Jesus with others. Our group became like a family to us.

By 1994, I began to sense that something was missing in our family. I had a growing relationship with the Lord, an incredible husband and two terrific sons, yet many times I would experience a moment where I reached for a child that wasn't there, or I would pick out three of something when I only needed two. It didn't take long to realize that the Lord was placing a desire for more children in my heart. It was also apparent to me that the Lord had **not** placed that same desire in my husband's heart.

Todd was busy building his new construction company. He was content with his family of four and had no desire for more children. As a matter of fact, whenever the subject came up he had a ready answer, "We have two healthy, happy sons. We don't need any more. God gave us two miracles. If you can guarantee me that you'll have a girl then we might have something to talk about!"

What made it worse for me was the fact that all my friends at church, who had started families after us, were having their third (or more) child. Each new baby that arrived elevated my desire for another child of our own. In an attempt to step in and take care of what I *thought* God had obviously forgotten to do, I tried several different approaches to change Todd's thinking about having more children.

The first approach was what I called the "baby saturation" approach. With so many babies being born all around us, I used every opportunity I could to get a baby into his arms. I hoped it would kick in some paternal hormone that would make him instantly change his mind. That didn't seem to work.

The second approach was a little subtler and required a lot of thinking and planning on my part. How many times in one day could I bring the word baby into the conversations we had? I even resorted to visual aides to help kick in that hormone of his. That didn't seem to work either.

The third approach was a last resort and was much more of an "in your face" approach. The term *nagging* might have been a more realistic term! I spent weeks trying to break through his wall of defense and cajole him into having another baby. That *definitely* didn't work.

For over a year I did everything I could to change Todd's heart. I was so frustrated with him and I just didn't understand why he objected to something I wanted so badly. But in one weekend, God changed my attitude and focus--from the inside out.

In the fall of 1994, our church held our annual women's retreat. That year we invited two gifted speakers to join us for the weekend retreat. They ministered mightily to our women, and it was a privilege to watch as God used them to bring healing and freedom.

After the Saturday morning session, I was in the worship center preparing for the afternoon session. The speakers were also getting ready, so we had the opportunity to visit. We had a wonderful time of fellowship, getting to know each other and sharing our hearts. I said nothing about my burning desire for another child. The afternoon session ended with a time of ministry, and as one of them prayed with some of the women, I sat quietly asking the Lord to either change Todd's heart or my desire. As I look back on that moment now, I realize that it was the first time I laid down my desires and allowed the Lord the opportunity to move. I had been trying to change Todd's heart on my own, without listening to the heart of my Heavenly Father.

That moment of releasing my desires and dreams to the Lord was a major turning point; I just didn't know it yet. As I sat watching ministry happening all around me, one of our speakers walked over to me. She knelt beside me and told me that the Lord had something to say to me.

I will always remember her next words, "Dana, The Lord says I know you. I know your desire, the desire for more children. I will give you the desires of your heart, but you need to trust Me. It may not be the way you think, but I **will** grant you the desire of your heart."

As tears rolled down my cheeks, I put my head on her shoulder. She quietly prayed over me and reassured me of God's grace and goodness. When she left, I sat there trying to allow the words to penetrate my head and more importantly, my heart. As I got up to get a drink of water a friend motioned me over to her. She told me she wanted to pray for me. She literally repeated word for word what the speaker had just said to me. It was an incredible moment of clarity. I went home with a supernatural peace I had longed to experience for two years. A peace that allowed me to give my heart's desire over to the One who was more than able to carry it. I knew that whatever the outcome might be, it was going to be okay because God was finally in control.

I didn't share what happened that weekend with anyone, not even Todd. I spent the next two weeks pondering and praying, trusting and believing that the Lord was much more capable than I would ever be to move in our lives and fulfill my heart's greatest desire. I was certainly not prepared for how quickly the Lord would move.

—⁂—

God, your Word says that you know me. You understand who I am and every thought and desire I have. I choose to trust you and I will ask for clarity, understanding and peace as I wait for your plans to come to pass. I am not alone.

The God Who Prepares Us

I Corinthians 2:9-10

For it is written, "What no eye has seen, what no ear has heard and what no mind has conceived- the things God has prepared for those who love him- these are the things God has revealed to us by His Spirit. The Spirit searches all things, even the deep things of God.

CHAPTER 4

November 8 I was getting ready that night for our weekly Bible study group. We were meeting at another couple's home for a potluck dinner and I was rushing around preparing the food.

Todd came into the kitchen, put his briefcase on the table and dropped the bombshell. "I called the Gladney Center today and ordered a packet on international adoptions from them. It's time to go get our daughter. What do you think about that?"

What did I think? What did I think? My mind was numb trying to process what he had just said, and I thought my heart was going to pop out of my chest.

All I could think to say was, "What made you do that?"

He looked at me slightly amused and quietly said, "I just thought it was time to bring your little girl home." Just like that. There it was. The words I had been waiting so long to hear. It had been less than five weeks since the retreat and God's promise to me had just become a reality. My daughter was on her way!

We have been asked by many people, *"Why China?"* There are a lot of reasons but the *real* reason is because that was where our daughter was! God knew her already because He had created her. He already had a purpose and a plan for her life and thankfully, His plan included us.

We both wanted a daughter and we knew something about the abundance of baby girls in China. Due to the one child per family laws in China at that time there were over 150,000 baby girls in orphanages throughout the country. With no social security system in place the responsibility of taking care of elderly parents fell on the sons. That reality created an environment where boys were considered more important than girls. It was a difficult situation for the families in China.

A friend suggested that I keep a journal recording every step of our journey to our daughter. It would be a written testimony to her that God had His hand in every detail and that a loving Father wonderfully and fearfully created her so that she could bless and enrich our family. That evening I began her story.

Journal entry:

My desire has always been to have a beautiful daughter, to hold and love; to shop with, paint nails and fix hair with. I long for the pleasure of watching her grow into a young woman and to be able to listen to her dream about her future, her hopes and visions and even her Prince Charming. Most importantly, I long to raise her up to be a Godly woman who loves the Lord with all her heart and who trusts Him to hold her hand through it all. You are the answer to this desire, and you will be a delightful treasure to Him and to us. Precious daughter- from this moment on you will NEVER be alone again.

I sat there with tears running down my face, tears of joy and thankfulness for the beautiful daughter that would grace our family. Each of our children had entered our lives in different and unique ways, and yet His mighty hand had crafted each of them. What a privilege it was to be part of that plan.

November 16 That night I asked the Lord for a Scripture that I could easily memorize and claim as a promise. As I opened my devotional book the Lord once again was quick to answer. The Scripture for that day was Matthew 18:1-5. Verse five jumped out at me as if bright headlights had been turned on in the room. In actuality they had; it was the light of illumination from the Holy Spirit. Such a simple verse yet it pierced my heart. "Whoever welcomes a little child like this in my name welcomes me". I highlighted the passage and went to bed thanking Him for the sweet answer He had provided.

November 22 After I put the boys to bed I felt the Lord calling me to pray for our daughter. I started with a general prayer, but before long I was praying specifically for her protection and safety. I sensed a need to go to battle for this baby that I had never laid eyes on; urged to war on her behalf. I spent over an hour praying for her that night. When I finished I opened my Bible and was led to Isaiah 46:3-4.

> Listen to me, O house of Jacob, all you who remain of the house of Israel. You whom I have upheld since you were conceived, and have carried since your birth. Even to your old age and gray hairs I am He, I am He who will sustain you. I have made you and I will sustain you and I will rescue you.

I didn't know the how or when of the journey ahead of us but there was one thing I knew for sure; I knew from that moment on God's will would be done. Our daughter would join our family in His timing and until she did He would be faithful to sustain her and keep her safe. He would indeed rescue her and place her lovingly into our waiting arms. The other Scripture the Lord showed me that evening was from Romans 5:3-5:

> We also rejoice in our sufferings, because we know that suffering produces perseverance, perseverance, character; and character, hope. And hope does not disappoint us, because God has poured out his love into our hearts by the Holy Spirit, whom he has given us.

I sensed the Lord telling me that on this journey there would be times when I would get discouraged, disappointed and frustrated. I knew He was reminding me that if I remembered to rejoice in each step that brought us closer to our daughter then hope would be our reward. It would be a hope that was undeniable and inextinguishable, a hope that would not be disappointed nor defeated. Never before had I experienced the Spirit's gift of faith as strongly as I did that night.

One of Todd's favorite sayings was, "God is preparing us for what He has prepared for us." That night I understood the saying on a much deeper level. God had been preparing us for this very moment in time. Each step of our lives up to this point had served a purpose and now all the preparation would result in an amazing gift, a gift that would bless us more than we could ever have imagined.

As I thought about our daughter I wondered what she looked like. I was glad to know that God knew exactly what she looked like, because He had created every part of her. We couldn't wait for the day to be able to hold her and call her ours. I had no idea in that moment what a roller coaster ride we were about to embark upon!

―⟿―

God, your Word says that as humans we can't begin to understand what you have prepared and planned for our lives. I choose to learn and earnestly seek to know who You are. I will seek you and draw close to you with my whole heart and obey your voice when you speak. I am not alone.

THE GOD WHO ORDERS ALL THINGS

Psalm 8:3-4

When I look at Your heavens, the work of Your fingers, the moon and the stars, which You have set in place, what is man that You are mindful of him, and the son of man that You care for him?

CHAPTER 5

December 1 Our packet on international adoptions arrived, and we began devouring the information. Any thoughts that we would just sign a few papers and be done quickly went out the window as I looked over what seemed to be a mountain of paperwork and legal documents required just to begin the process. After reading about foreign dossiers, home studies, INS pre-approval forms, and formal applications, I quickly surmised that we needed to attend the orientation meeting that Gladney offered for prospective clients. Unfortunately, the next orientation was not scheduled until the middle of January. I felt a sense of urgency about completing this adoption and knew it was a prompting from the Holy Spirit. I told Todd that night that I didn't think we should wait until January to get started. He just nodded and said, "Do what you need to do."

I called the next morning and spoke to Charlotte, Gladney's International Program Coordinator for Chinese adoptions. I had no idea at the time what a wonderful friend and advocate we would have in her. Over the long months that were to follow, she and the rest of the staff would work tirelessly on our behalf and they would never waver in their support. After visiting with Charlotte over the phone I was able to arrange a private orientation the following week. I spent much of that weekend praying for God's wisdom to be able to organize all the required documentation as quickly as possible. I tend to operate most effectively when everything is orderly and neat. Most of the time my organizational skills are a blessing, but sometimes they can be detrimental and this was one of those times. It was extremely frustrating because I was ready to get all my ducks in a row, but I did not know where my ducks were or what order they were supposed to be in!

December 5 *My Rainbow in the Cloud* – That was the title of the daily devotional I read that morning as I spent time with the Lord. Both Joshua and Jacob had special names I had given them when they were little: Joshua was my sunshine and Jacob, my angel. We had all wondered what our daughter's special name would be, and the boys had fun trying to guess. Their ideas ranged from moonshine (I didn't even try to explain that one to them!) all the way to sugarplum. But as soon as I saw the title of my devotional that morning the Holy Spirit clearly spoke to me saying, *"This is her special name."*

My rainbow--how perfect! Just as God put a rainbow in the sky after the flood as a promise to Noah, she would be the fulfillment of God's promise to us. She would bring an array of beautiful, vibrant colors into our home. Her life would shine brilliantly as a reminder to all those who would meet her of the love and devotion our Heavenly Father has for each of us. She would be a true reflection of God's grace, mercy and unconditional love.

December 11 Orientation day! We met Charlotte and she instantly put us at ease. After walking us through the preliminaries of international adoptions, she gave us the specifics of how to work through all the paperwork. She even gave me a flowchart to help organize it all. A flowchart? My appreciation for her skyrocketed with that piece of organizational heaven! After visiting with her for over an hour my heart was racing. I couldn't wait to get started. She told us that the time frame for adopting from China varied, but at the current time we would most likely travel to China within six months. The possibility of having our daughter in that short a time was so exciting to us.

As we prepared to leave, Charlotte invited us to a Christmas party for families that had already, or were currently in the process of, adopting internationally. The party would be at a home about five minutes from ours. When she gave us the directions I looked at Todd in amazement. We quickly realized that it was not just *any* home. We knew this home VERY well. We spent many days in that home with the people who originally built it, two of the most important people in our lives, Bill and Marianne Flanders. They were not just close friends to us; they were counselors, confidants, teachers, and the most incredible examples of what an authentic Christian couple looks like.

The party being in this home was no coincidence; it was a kiss from God. We would begin our journey in a home that we knew had been built and firmly established on the foundation of an Almighty God. A home that held so many wonderful memories of lessons learned and guidance shared. We left that meeting confident of the decision the Lord had led us to; confident that He was in every detail and that we were moving in His will.

As soon as we got home that afternoon I got busy. I got the flow chart out and started making notes and plans all over it. Charlotte had given us names, addresses, and phone numbers for all the state and governmental agencies needed to obtain the required legal documents.

It was very time consuming to prepare the documents. Each document had to be authenticated, which meant that the documents issued in the U.S. would be legally acceptable in China. Each document had to be an original and true copy. We had to have each document notarized, sent on to the state where it was originally issued to have a state seal attached to it, then finally sent to the nearest foreign embassy to be authenticated there. All this had to be done in duplicate. When completed, we needed three copies of each original. That flow chart was a lifesaver!

My first call was to the state of New York, my birth state. Charlotte had warned us that working with the state of New York might be quite a challenge and that the red tape could be exasperating at times, so I was prepared for the battle. I called the phone number she had given us and was connected to a wonderful lady named Jan. As I shared my excitement about our journey she quickly became very interested and supportive. I asked her how to begin the process of obtaining an original of my birth certificate. She paused for a moment and then told me to hold on for a minute.

A few minutes later she came back on the line and said, "Okay, here's what we do. Give me the information on your birth certificate. I am right next door to all the offices you need. I will pull your certificate and take it to the proper offices for you. Send me a pre-addressed Fed Ex envelope today, and I will have it all ready to send back to you tomorrow."

I had to smile as I hung up the phone. Although it was hard to believe that a total stranger would be so willing to help I wasn't really surprised. God was in charge and His order would not be denied!

December 16 Before heading to the Gladney Christmas Party in Southlake, we went by our local police department to be fingerprinted. The boys took cookies for the officers and we had a friend videotape it all for us. Todd had decided to video the journey as well to have yet another record for our daughter. We wanted her to know just how special she was to us. When we were finished at the police station, we went to the party and had a wonderful time. We met many people who had already adopted from Russia, Paraguay, and, of course, China. Todd and I just sat in awe watching the little girls from China running in and out of the rooms in their Christmas dresses with matching hair bows. They were so beautiful! You could see the joy of life just beaming from their faces as they giggled and squealed the whole night. Their proud parents were beaming as well and eager to share their wisdom and knowledge with us. It was a wonderful evening for our entire family.

It was important to Todd and I that the boys were involved in every part of the journey to our daughter. We didn't want them to ever feel left out of this life-changing event in our family. The boys had a lot of fun getting to see all the children and by the time we left, the boys were filled with just as much excitement and expectation as Todd and I.

That night as I slept I had a dream where I saw myself in a room and I was holding a beautiful, dark-skinned baby in my arms. I was talking quietly to her as she cooed and smiled. As the dream progressed, I saw that I was putting a beautiful red velvet dress on her. When I held her in my arms, she had the biggest smile on her face and started to wave her hand up and down. The joy I felt in my spirit was so overwhelming that I woke up with tears streaming down my face. That dream was so clear and so real that I saw it over and over again in my mind over the months to follow. I even went to the store and bought a red velvet dress and shiny black patent leather shoes.

Our entire family was so full of anticipation and enthusiasm. We just knew that God was going to move quickly to bring our daughter home to us. I was blissfully unaware of how different our timing and God's perfect timing would be!

―――∞―――

God your Word says that your hand set the moon and stars in place and that all things are put in order through you. I choose to believe that your hand will order my life as well, and I trust that the end result will be as beautiful and endless as the stars that you so carefully placed in the sky. I am not alone.

The God Who Sings over Us

Zephaniah 3:17

The Lord your God is with you, the Mighty Warrior who saves. He will take great delight in you; in His love He will no longer rebuke you, but will rejoice over you with singing.

CHAPTER 6

The next month, nearly every waking moment was spent obtaining the needed legal documents and completing the Gladney application. We had to get physical exams, collect referral letters, obtain criminal record checks by the local police, compile a personal assets inventory, send off for passports, as well as get statements of good standing from our bank and a letter from our C.P.A. verifying our financial stability. There were also many, many trips to Federal Express and a lot of time spent on the phone to different governmental agencies. Through it all, I continued to have a sense of urgency about finishing my part of the process and getting the completed dossier off to China.

By the end of January I completed all the paperwork and sent our application to Gladney. I gathered all the documents that were going to go to the Chinese Consulate in Houston for their authentication and made one more trip to the local Federal Express drop box. The boys and I gathered around in a circle placed our hands on the package and prayed over it before we slipped it into the slot. This had become a routine with the three of us, praying over each packet of documents that went out. We would pray the Lord's hand of protection over it, that we would have favor in the eyes of the person who would process the request, and that the Lord would move the paperwork through quickly. It was a wonderful reminder to us that the Lord was in control at all times and that His will would be done. The next few weeks there was nothing for us to do but wait.

With the paperwork done, we turned our attention to an amazing twelve-day trip that Todd and I were going on to Israel. Todd's parents were taking a group of people on a tour and we were so excited to be going with them.

The Stone's had gone to Israel many times on personal trips and recently had begun taking groups of people on biblically based tours that helped strengthen the understanding of a Christian's Jewish roots. Because of all the wonderful things we had heard about these trips, we knew it would be a life-changing experience. Todd loved traveling and he relished the time leading up to those trips. He would spend weeks researching the places we would visit. Understandably, he was really excited to be going on this trip. All I could think about was going to China!

We also had to keep in close contact with Gladney during that time. They had so many families close to completing their dossiers that they were going to have to send them in two groups. The first group of documents would be sent to China at the end of February. Once approved, that group of families would travel to China in late April. The second group of dossiers would be sent in mid-April with those families traveling in mid-July. Because our trip to Israel was planned for late April, Charlotte suggested that we wait to be part of the second group.

I continued to have the strong sense of urgency to move quickly and I fretted for several days. Then one night, the Lord reminded me that one of the most important lessons we can learn is the value of being content as we wait. Psalm 130:5-7 says,

> "I wait for the Lord, my soul waits, and in his
> Word I put my hope."

I chose that night to put my trust and my HOPE in the One whose unfailing love would bring His promise to fruition. That night I put our daughter totally into God's hands and trusted Him to work out the rest. It was a lesson I would learn again and again through the journey to our daughter.

February 15 It had been just two months since we started the adoption document process, and I now held in my hands the completed, authenticated documents. All that remained was for a Gladney representative to come out for our home study. I called Charlotte and set up an appointment for March 1. She also had great news about all the dossiers being sent to China. The Chinese New Year had fallen in mid-February that year, so Gladney had delayed sending over any of the dossiers, so ours would be in the first group going over. Of course that meant we had to consider the possibility of going straight from Israel to China. I tried to figure out how to pack for two trips plus baby supplies in limited luggage. Todd and I spent several long nights packing and repacking, trying to find the perfect balance of clothes and supplies!

March 1 Charlotte came out that morning to conduct our home study. It consisted of joint and individual interviews with Todd and me, as well as talking to the boys and examining the house. We had a great time visiting with her, and she was able to hear firsthand about our lives, our beliefs and our desire to add a daughter to our family. After a two-hour visit, she gathered us all together and informed us that we had been officially approved to adopt a daughter from China. Things were moving along so well. Our anticipation grew more and more each day.

The following day Charlotte called to tell me that she was going to walk our final papers through so they could send our dossier over with the first group that month. We were thrilled; everything was coming together. Thoughts of nurseries, diapers, clothes, bottles and bassinets filled our heads as we finally allowed ourselves to start imagining life with a new baby in the house. We went to church that Sunday, and during prayer and praise time we shared the news with our church family. I pictured in my mind the time when I would walk into church holding our beautiful little girl in that red velvet dress. What a joyous day that would be!

March 14 As I sat down that night to spend some time with the Lord, He gave me a gift that I had waited three months to receive; a song for my daughter. I was so excited because God had recently given me a gift of hearing songs of love that He was singing over certain people. It was a gift I had received a few months earlier when Todd and I went skiing with other couples on a Worship/Ski Retreat at Crested Butte, Colorado. The couple that organized the retreat was Dennis and Melinda Jernigan. Dennis is an incredibly gifted man who ministers to people all around the world through songs the Lord gives to him. He is known as a modern day psalmist. He hears the songs that the Lord sings over people; songs that refresh, renew, and restore minds and spirits.

Each night at the retreat Dennis led worship in a small church next door to our hotel named the O Be Joyful Church; and joyful we were. We spent hours singing songs that Dennis had written. One evening he asked if any of us wanted to receive the gift of hearing the Lord's songs in their own lives. I immediately stood to my feet and as Dennis prayed over us the presence of the Lord filled that room. Within a week, I began to hear those songs. It wasn't that I could audibly hear them, but instead words and melodies would come to my mind at different times. It was an incredibly powerful experience. It was an honor to be able to speak His words of encouragement and love to others.

So that night in March, when the Lord revealed the song He was singing over my daughter's life, I was moved beyond words. The words went like this,

From the day you were formed, by our Heavenly Lord
You've been loved by this Daddy and Mom.
We have waited and prayed, for that one special day
When we'd hold you and call you our own.
And when the sun breaks through, and God brings you,
You'll be our little rainbow of love; you'll be our little rainbow of love.

I stayed up until midnight putting the lyrics and melody on paper. I was so thankful for such a beautiful song to share with my daughter as she grew. The Lord had given me songs for both the boys, and I sang those songs to them each night before we said prayers. It was such a special way to end the day and they loved hearing them. The boys even made me record them so if Todd and I ever went out of town they would still be able to listen to their song. It was a daily reminder to them that they were special, loved, and uniquely created by God. And now our daughter would have that same assurance.

The following week the Lord gave me the second verse to her song. It was another reminder that His promise to me would be realized, and that one day I would be able to hold her in my arms:

> *Now we're holding you tight, what a heavenly sight*
> *No more waiting or wanting you so.*
> *You are loved and adored, by our heavenly Lord,*
> *And your family who wants you to know.*
> *That the sun broke through,*
> *When God brought you*
> *Our little rainbow of love,*
> *You're our little rainbow of love.*

I wrote in her journal that night that God would be victorious, no matter what difficult circumstances or situations might arise during our journey to her. Unfortunately, those difficult circumstances were about to begin.

God, your Word says that You take great delight in me and that You love singing over my life. I choose to lay the worries of the day down and listen quietly for Your voice. I will spend time with You and allow Your songs of love to penetrate my heart and bring healing to my soul. I am not alone.

THE GOD WHO CALLS US BY NAME

Isaiah 43:1

But now says the Lord, He who created you, O Jacob, He who formed you, O Israel: Do not fear, for I have redeemed you; I have called you by name, you are Mine.

CHAPTER 7

March 21 Charlotte had called us a few days earlier to tell us that they had not received our I.N.S. approval letter. It was Wednesday and Gladney was planning to send the completed dossiers out the following Monday. My heart fell when I hung up the phone and I quickly asked the Lord for help. Within an hour the doorbell rang and standing there was the Fed Ex lady I had gotten to know very well over the last few months. In her hands was the package containing our I.N.S. approval letter. All I needed to do now was send the letter overnight to the Chinese Consulate in Houston to get authenticated and stamped with their approval.

I called Charlotte back and she told me to address the return air bill to the Gladney offices so they would have the completed document in their hands first thing Monday morning. I rushed it over to the Fed Ex drop box, took a deep breath and as I prayed I gave thanks for the Lord's continued hand in every single detail. The package would arrive in Houston Thursday and be returned to Gladney on Friday, well ahead of their deadline. The crisis had been averted.

Monday morning I called Charlotte to make sure she had received the package. Her response stopped me in my tracks, "No, Dana, I'm sorry but it didn't come." I told her I would track the package and get right back to her. My hands were shaking as I called Fed Ex and had them track the missing package. The man on the other end of the line came back on the phone and said, "Well, I don't know how this happened, but your package seems to be in Wichita, Kansas."

"Kansas? Kansas!" I said. "How in the world is my package in Kansas?" I tried to explain the deadline we were facing and the importance of that package being delivered today to its intended destination. "Lady, I'm sorry, but there is no way that package is getting there today," was his only response. I hung up the phone frustrated and disappointed. I knew when I called Charlotte back to tell her that the package wouldn't be there on time that she would say we could wait until the next group of dossiers was sent. That sense of urgency began welling up within me again so I did the one thing I knew to do, I prayed. I asked the Lord to give me wisdom in how to handle the situation, I asked for favor and then I thanked Him for going before me to make the path smooth. When I called Charlotte back I explained the situation to her. She was quiet for a minute before she said, "Dana, just get the package here. I will wait for it before I send this group."

I thanked her and hung up the phone. I knew that the enemy had volleyed his first attack and God had intervened. I sat there with my hand on the phone for a few minutes quietly thanking the Lord for this victory. The next day our package arrived safely at Gladney. We breathed a sigh of relief. Our dossier was finally on its way to China. We spent the next three weeks getting ready for our trip to Israel. We were able to enjoy the anticipation of all we would experience there because we weren't worrying about the adoption.

There was one *very* special adoption related item that I looked forward to finding in Israel--our daughter's name. Since we began the adoption process I had tried to get Todd to talk about a name for our daughter. Naming our children was very important to us because we believe that a person's name is significant and speaks into who they will be. We spent much time in prayer over Joshua and Jacob's names, but every time I asked Todd about our daughter's name he would always say the same thing, "God will show us her name in Israel."

Sometimes I pushed him to at least consider options. He would just laugh and say, "How about something with an Asian feel to it, like Jade?" Beyond that, he would not talk about it. So I was looking forward to being able to call our daughter by her God provided name. Little did I know how accurate those words would be!

April 21 We had finally arrived in Israel! We didn't know it at the time but that same day our dossier was being delivered to the Chinese authorities in Beijing. After a long eleven-hour flight from New York to Tel Aviv we boarded our tour bus to make our way to the hotel for the night. As we rode through the beautiful country listening to our guide we relaxed, enjoying the view. Suddenly, something he said made me sit straight up in my seat and spin around to look at Todd. He was sitting there with tears in his eyes and at that moment we both knew. The Lord had just revealed our daughter's name to us.

The guide was telling us about the town where we would spend the night. "Tonight," he said, "we will spend the night in the town of Netanya; which means provided by God."

Netanya.

Netanya.

The name just kept rolling through my heart like waves on the ocean. I tried to imagine the beautiful face that would go with the name the Lord had picked out especially for her.

Over the next few days we would add the name Jade as her middle name. Todd had joked so often about the name Jade that I finally looked up the meaning; it meant *priceless one.* Netanya Jade, our God provided priceless one. That night the Lord gave us James 1:17 that would become her life verse,

> Every good and perfect gift comes from above from the Father of heavenly lights, who does not change like shifting shadows.

And a perfect gift she would be! The trip was everything we had hoped for and so much more. It was a life changing two weeks. We learned so much about the land and the people of Israel. We saw many of the places where Jesus walked, preached and ministered. It was an incredible experience and it deepened our walk with the Lord in ways I could never have imagined. We were more thankful than ever that our names were written in the Lamb's Book of Life and that God Himself knew each of them. We came home with a much better understanding of why that tiny nation is so special and why we should each be in continual prayer for it and its people.

May 5 We returned home from Israel in the evening and after reuniting with the boys and getting everyone settled in, I sat down to thumb through the mail. A letter from Gladney caught my eye. I opened it up hoping for some great news. What I read was definitely news, but it was not great at all. The letter informed us that due to U.S. sanctions levied against China, the Chinese government had temporarily closed the doors to American adoptions while they decided what their response to the sanctions would be. Closed the doors? What did that mean for us and for our daughter? I was too tired to even think straight so as we crawled into bed, we did the best thing we could do. We prayed. Together, we put it all in the Lord's hands and went to sleep with peaceful hearts.

The next morning I called Charlotte. Her voice was cheery and upbeat which instantly put me at ease. "Dana, I'm glad you called. The day before yesterday China reopened the doors to adoptions. They are proceeding as usual with all the adoptions." I couldn't help but ask, "What effect do you think all of this will have on our adoption?" Her response was encouraging, "I really think the delay will only put you maybe a month behind where you were. We're hoping July will be your month."

That would give me time to finish school with the boys and get Netanya's nursery ready. Perfect timing because Netanya's nursery was the next thing to tackle on that flowchart of mine!

The nursery theme had been easy to decide. What better picture of God's rainbow promise than the story of Noah and his ark? I searched for a border that was a traditional Noah's Ark pattern with burgundy, dark blue and hunter green as the primary colors. That proved to be quite a challenge. If I found the right colors the pattern looked like a cartoon. If I found a traditional pattern, the colors were wrong! I was turning into a typical nesting mommy to-be! Todd and Joshua finally found something they thought I would like at a local store so I scurried off to look for myself. Of course, it was perfect. After I ordered the border I went on the search for the perfect crib set. These things are important to us moms!

My mom called me that night with news that she had found the "perfect" Christmas stocking for Netanya. Mom had a long held tradition of needle pointing stockings for each of her grandchildren. Netanya would be number nine. It was a true labor of love for her and she enjoyed every moment of it. She would spend weeks scouring through hundreds of options trying to find just the right one for each grandchild and then work for months to complete each one. She said she loved spending time praying for each baby "with every knot I tie".

She was so excited as she began, "Dana, I went to the store to look for a stocking kit for Netanya. I found one that was really cute, but it didn't seem very "Christmassy", so I put it back. I spent an hour looking at a lot of other ones but I kept being drawn back to that first one. I spent almost two hours in that store trying to decide which one to get, but I just kept going back to the first one so I finally decided Christmassy or not, I was going to get it!"

After that explanation, I was anxious to know what it was about that stocking that kept drawing her back to it. She explained, "Like I said, it doesn't have anything to do with Christmas but… it's a Noah's Ark with a beautiful rainbow across the top."

"Mom," I said, "You are going to love the story I am about to share with you!" When I shared the story of how the Lord had given me Netanya's love name she started to cry. She was so excited that the Lord had spoken to her too!

That Sunday after church we went to a Gladney International Families picnic at a nearby park. It was a gorgeous day in May and we had a wonderful time meeting new families and visiting again with those who had been at the Christmas party. Todd and I loved watching all the children running and playing without seeming to have a care in the world. It was hard to imagine what these children's lives had been and but for the hand of a loving God, would have continued to be. The only difficult part for us was not having our daughter there yet. We felt somewhat lonely and empty. Everyone there kept telling us how special this time of waiting was. Easy for *them* to say I thought! They heard the squeals of delight as they pushed their child higher and higher on the swings and as they washed ketchup and chocolate chip cookies off ten beautiful fingers. We had to sit and watch. All I wanted was to have someone put my daughter into my arms. Waiting was not always easy.

God, your Word says that You know me and that You redeemed me. You call me by name, because I am Your child. I choose to allow You to be my Father. I can always trust that as my Father, You will be here for me and watch over me at all times. I am not alone.

The God Who Battles for Us

Isaiah 41:10

Do not fear, for I am with you, do not be afraid, for I am your God; I will strengthen you, I will help you, I will uphold you with My victorious right hand.

CHAPTER 8

May 29 My spirit was heavy. It was so heavy for a few days that I had a hard time focusing on anything else. It felt as if something was getting ready to happen and it wasn't going to be good. I spent several days irritable and angry without really knowing why. All I could do was ask the Lord to give me His wisdom and help me understand why I felt like I did. Unfortunately, a late afternoon phone call to Charlotte brought the answer.

Charlotte told me that effective immediately the Beijing National Government had switched the roles of the two national bureaus that handled international adoptions. They hoped that the switch would eliminate duplication of efforts between the two ministries and streamline the adoption process. But what did that mean for us? It meant more waiting and more uncertainty. I hung up not quite sure what all that meant, but I was confident that Gladney was on top of it.

We received a follow up letter a few days later that tried to explain the effects in more detail. The letter told us that because of the switch the bureaus would need time to hire new staff, learn the duties they were now responsible for, and most importantly work their way through the over 800 cases already in process. With that many cases we would most likely have an additional four to six month wait. All the staff at Gladney could say was that we were going to have to be patient and pray. They were working overtime trying to keep the lines of communication open with the two bureaus and initiate new contacts. I knew then why my spirit had been so heavy. The enemy was gearing up for his second attack.

Surprisingly enough after reading the letter there was no sinking feeling, fear or despair. Instead there was determination and confidence in the Lord's plan for our family. Gone was the heavy feeling. I knew what it was time to do, go to battle in prayer for my daughter.

I opened my Bible to pull out a Scripture that the Lord had given me the day before. When I read it initially I had no idea why He had given it to me or what its significance was, but I knew now! The Scripture was Isaiah 55:5,

> Surely you will summon nations you know not, and nations that do not know you will hasten to you, because of the Lord your God, the Holy One of Israel, has endowed you with His splendor.

As I began to pray I knew I had the mightiest weapon of all, the Word of God. For the first time in my life I knew what it felt like to be an intercessor. God had given me my assignment and the words to use. A boldness rose up within me that I had never felt before. I typed up that Scripture and printed out about thirty copies. All our friends at church were constantly asking if there was anything they could specifically pray for us. Now I could say yes.

I took the copies to our sons' baseball games that night. I went up and down the row handing them out and told our friends to get busy knocking the enemy off his feet. We knew we could count on our close-knit group of friends for anything. They would definitely pray, and I was confident that God would respond.

I will never know what was happening in the life of my daughter at that moment. She had not even been born yet, but I knew that God had His hand on her and somehow protected her from harm.

June 1 A new song from the Lord that reminded me of the power He possesses and the peace He brings.

> *"When my enemy surrounds me, I will not fear.*
> *Though the war breaks out against me, I know my Lord is near.*
> *In the day of tribulation, He will keep me safe,*
> *He will hide me in His dwelling place, when I seek Him face to face.*
> *So I will wait and be strong, I will wait and take heart,*
> *I will wait upon the Lord.*
> *Yes, I will wait and be strong; I will wait and take heart,*
> *I will wait upon the Lord."*

Yes, I would wait and be strong. My trust in the Lord was rock solid. I knew that the wait would produce the desires of my heart. I just needed to be patient for His timing and stay in His presence. The great news was that while we waited we had a lot of life going on in our family!

Between baseball, swimming, Vacation Bible School, and visits to Grandma's house, the summer filled quickly. It wasn't until later that I realized that all the busyness and all the activity was a blessing from the Lord. With so much going on it helped keep my mind off my empty arms. God's timing was being perfected. We were content to wait upon Him.

July 3 Another letter from Gladney arrived. As I opened the letter that day I sat down and took a deep breath. The letter contained a detailed update on the changes that were continuing to take place between the two bureaus in China. It also tried to answer the "how much longer?" question for the families involved. There were so many of us who were in different stages of the process that I knew it must have been difficult for the staff to answer that question and remain positive, yet realistic. The information concerning our adoption fell into the "nothing-new" category.

When I was almost at the end of the letter something at the bottom of the page caught my eye. Gladney was sending several staff members to China on a humanitarian aid and fact-finding trip. They wanted to meet some of the new officials in charge and hand deliver seven more dossiers. While they were there, they also wanted to hand deliver donations of clothing, medicine and toys to show their support and concern for the orphanages they worked with. What they needed from all of us were the actual items. Instantly the Lord placed an idea in my head, and I knew just where to go to collect those much needed items.

Our church had a heart for children. The members were a giving, loving group of people who were just waiting for the chance to help someone. I called our pastor and told him about the opportunity. He didn't hesitate. He told me that I could go before the congregation the following Sunday, present the need and allow God to move.

Our church was blessed to have a pastor who daily sought God's face and was willing to step out and move when God told him to. He and his wife were our spiritual rocks during this journey. Whenever we felt defeated, frustrated or impatient they were always there with a hug, a prayer and a word of encouragement.

That Sunday I stood before our church family and shared my heart. I told them of the thousands of children in the orphanages and the opportunity we had to bless those children. I told them that our daughter was one of the thousands that needed their love and support.

The following Wednesday I went to the church to gather whatever donations had been collected. When I walked into the lobby I couldn't believe my eyes. Boxes were everywhere! There were hundreds of bottles of medicine, shampoo, baby toys, clothing and diapers. There were so many donations that I had to take all the seats out of my Suburban just to fit them all in. It was literally packed to the top by the time everything had been loaded. But that wasn't all.

While I was loading all the boxes in my car the financial secretary called me into her office and told me that there had also been several cash donations. She smiled and handed me a check for over $2,300. Words could not express the gratitude that was in my heart. When I arrived at Gladney they were stunned! It took six staff members to help get everything inside. Many of the other staff members came out just to look. What an incredible witness our church had provided for this amazing group of people. Charlotte was speechless when I handed her the check and she decided that it would be used to buy antibiotics when they got to China. I drove away with a heart bursting with pride at how the Body of Christ came together and was so willing to answer when the Lord called them to action.

That night during my devotional time, the Lord reminded me that His plans and purposes for our lives are so much bigger than we could ever fathom. Our life journey is like a movie filmed on one of those old-fashioned movie reels. Because we are human our view is often limited to one frame at a time. Our lives seem to move slowly and the frame-by-frame view can be confusing and difficult to follow with changes almost imperceptible at times. But God, as the producer and director of our lives sees the completed work. When the frames begin to flow together they create a beautiful masterpiece of our lives worthy of the greatest of honors. Our assignment is to trust and listen to His direction, to move when He asks us to move and to be content when He asks us to rest and be still. He allowed me to see the frames in this portion of our movie that day.

I saw the faces of hundreds of children that were going to be blessed with desperately needed supplies. I understood that if we had breezed through this adoption process, if there were no delays or periods of waiting we would never have had the opportunity to be a part of this blessing that would benefit so many of God's precious little ones. God saw the whole picture, and He allowed us to be a small part of it. Before the next few weeks were over I would be crying out to the Lord to see the end of this movie.

God, your Word says that I am not to be afraid, because You will battle on my behalf. I choose to stand strong when fear grips me. I will rest in the knowledge that the victory has already been won, and You will be here to strengthen and help me through every situation and circumstance. I am not alone.

The God Who Gives Us Peace

John 14:27

Peace I leave with you; My peace I give you. I do not give to you as the world gives. Do not let your hearts be troubled and do not be afraid.

CHAPTER 9

August 16 Joshua's ninth birthday. It started off full of excitement and anticipation. My birthday was the following day, so my mom was coming in from San Antonio and my brother and his family was coming in from Ft. Hood. We were all going to a Texas Rangers baseball game on Saturday to celebrate both of the birthdays.

As I scanned through the mail that afternoon I found yet another letter from Gladney. I remember thinking: *This is it. God has arranged for our referral to come just in time for my birthday. Isn't that JUST like God?* I tore open the envelope ready to read the good news; instead what I read almost broke my heart.

The letter stated that the Chinese government had decided to give full control of International adoptions to the China Center for Adoption Affairs (CCAA), which was under the Ministry of Civil Affairs. The Gladney staff members who had gone to China the previous month attended several meetings with the CCAA. The letter highlighted the main changes that would take place. Phrases such as *no estimates on how long*, *several hundred backlogged cases*, and *could be another seven months to a year,* flooded my quickly numbing mind. But it was what I read next that really broke my heart.

The CCAA has decided to strictly apply Chinese law and expresses that it will not be lenient regarding referrals of children to families who do not meet the 35 years of age and/or childless criteria. Families who do not meet these criteria must be open to considering a child with a significant handicap. Past agreements, which allowed for a more lenient child referral system, are not expected to continue. Those families who do not meet the criteria but want to test the new system are certainly encouraged to do so. Please be aware that you may be forced to wait over a year and still not be offered a referral in the end. If you do not feel comfortable doing this, you may want to consider transferring your file to another country like Vietnam.

Vietnam? But our daughter was in China! My heart and mind flooded with emotions as I sat on the couch trying not to cry. The boys had friends over, and they were sitting right in front of me playing on the floor. I knew I couldn't react emotionally so I quietly prayed for the Lord to still my heart and remove the fear welling up within me. It terrified me to think that this might be the death of our vision. It took everything in me to get up off the couch and make one more phone call to Charlotte.

All she could say was that I would need to wait and call back when the Vice President of International Adoptions was back in the office. She had been the one who met with the officials in China, and she could give me more specific details concerning our individual case. Until then all we could do was wait and pray.

Wait. There was that word again. Wait. I was so beginning to hate that word. I didn't want to wait one more second. In that moment I gave in to my emotions. I slammed the phone down, went to my room and threw what can best be described as a temper tantrum. I gave in to the anger, the hurt and confusion. Why was this so hard? Why did God promise me a daughter and then make each step so agonizing?

I sat on my bathroom floor for over an hour and complained to God. His response? Silence. Nothing. There was no reply. Finally, I had no more tears. I crawled up on our bed and rested for a while.

I finally got up, fixed my make up and put a smile on my face, although I was still fussing at the Lord. Somehow I managed to make it through the rest of the day without letting anyone know how I was truly feeling. I waited until everyone had gone to bed that night to show Todd the letter. Thankfully, His faith would not be shaken. His response was simply, "Dana, things change every day over there! We need to just wait and see what happens. Tomorrow it could be a totally different story." He sounded so confident that it gave me the much-needed peace I had been missing all day. We prayed before we went to bed and asked the Lord to give us the strength we needed to wait on His timing.

We spent the next day going to the Rangers game, celebrating birthdays and relaxing. The busyness was good but my mind continually wandered back to the letter and the ramifications that might result from all the changes. Sunday morning we all went to church. I had decided to make sure I put on a happy face, because I knew if I gave over to my emotions again I wouldn't make it through the service. But God had other plans for me. As soon as worship started I felt the presence of God all around me. It was so strong that I had to sit down in my seat. The overwhelming feeling of His love and mercy washed over me time and time again. I cried through the entire service releasing the frustrations and fears that had besieged me over the last two days. Our pastor kept looking down at me trying, I am sure, to figure out what in the world was going on, but all I could do was cry.

Our altars were always open for prayer at the end of each service, and I knew I needed to go. It felt like I was crawling on my hands and knees as I made my way there and began to quietly pour my heart out to the Lord. Then I felt the familiar hands of my pastor envelope mine. He had no idea what was wrong, and all he could do was put his arms around me and hug me. But they weren't his arms that I felt encircling me, they were the Lord's. There was a peace and an assurance in those arms that day. I knew the Lord was reaching down and holding me letting me know it was all going to be okay, letting me know He was there and that He hadn't left me--not for a minute. I heard Todd praying behind me, and I could sense many hands on me. But all I truly felt was the warm presence of God.

After a few minutes I began to feel His strength become my strength and His peace become my peace. He was restoring my faith. My mother was standing behind me quietly singing. As I stood up she took me in her arms and told me how much she loved me. Then she said, "Dana, in all things, remember to give thanks to the Lord. Why don't we do that right know? Let's give Him praise for all He has done and all He is going to do!" So we stood at the altar, arms raised up, singing and giving thanks. It was a total act of surrender. I wanted Him to know that no matter what happened from that day forward I would trust Him, I would honor Him and I would always be thankful that He was by my side. He had allowed my tears, my anger and my sorrow, and then He had picked me up and lovingly put me back on solid ground to walk in His strength.

That night I wrote in Netanya's journal:

Journal entry:

So with God's grace and peace, and with the strong, NEVER wavering faith that your Dad has, we keep walking. We KNOW that God has given you to us, and now we WILL wait for His timing to be made perfect in this latest struggle. God's hand is continually on you, Netanya, and His protection will keep you safe 'even to your old age and gray hairs,' until you are safely in our arms. Before long I will be able to sing the line to you from your song, 'no more waiting or wanting you so. And before long that red velvet dress will be yours.'

I called Gladney the next week to get first hand information from the VP. She told me that the letter had been correct in all its facts, but we should not give up hope. Sometimes what was stated in those meetings did not necessarily become reality. Her advice was for us to test the system and to continue on in the process until someone told us differently. We talked for a while about other countries like Vietnam, but I told her we were set on China. We were prepared to wait it out. I hung up knowing that God had just carried me through one of the darkest places of our journey to Netanya. I was so thankful that I didn't have to walk through it on my own.

—⁂—

God your Word says that You give me a peace that no one else can. I choose to ignore the worries of the world and any sadness that I might experience and allow my heart, my mind and my spirit to experience the true peace that can only come from You. I am not alone.

The God Who Watches over Us

Psalm 33:18

*But the eyes of the Lord are on all those who fear Him,
on those whose hope is in His unfailing love.*

CHAPTER 10

Over the next two months we waited and each day we hoped the phone would ring. Our church family shared the wait with us. Netanya was not just ours anymore; she was going to belong to them too. Every day someone would inevitably ask, "Any news?" or "What's the latest?" It was comforting to know that we had literally hundreds of people praying for our daughter every day, not just at our church but also around the United States. Family and friends had their churches praying, and they were just as anxious as we were for that phone to ring.

There were some days when there would be a twinge of heartache when those questions would be asked and I would have to reply, "No, nothing, we are still waiting," but I knew beyond a shadow of a doubt that God's plan would be fulfilled in our family. We weren't walking this path alone. God had His hand on one shoulder and our friends had their hands on the other. It was the sweetest gift of love I have ever felt.

I started our fifth year of homeschooling that fall. Joshua was in the fourth grade and Jacob was in kindergarten. Joshua would do independent work in the morning while I worked with Jacob then they would switch in the afternoons. I was also busy because I volunteered to be the director of the Tarrant County Operation Christmas Child (OCC) Collection Center. Our church participated in this very worthwhile ministry the previous year, and I served as the coordinator. I had been so blessed by the experience that I volunteered to make our church a collection center for all of Tarrant County. It was a massive undertaking, but I loved every minute of it.

The ministry is part of Samaritan's Purse headed by Franklin Graham. The concept is so simple yet has an eternal impact. People are asked to fill shoeboxes full of gifts: toys, school supplies, hygiene products, candy, etc. The gift-filled shoeboxes are then sent to children in war-torn areas all around the world as well as to areas that have experienced natural disasters or areas of extreme poverty. Just seeing the pictures of children receiving these shoeboxes was enough to make me want to do anything I could to help. What a simple yet powerful way it was to share the love of Jesus with His most cherished possession, his children.

The Collection Center was going to be open for two weeks in November, but the work involved in getting the word out and arranging for all the details of the process was time consuming. It took the better part of the three months prior to the actual opening to prepare properly. Life was full and again God provided me with a wonderful opportunity to help minister to hurting children. It was yet another frame that God was using to create the finished story for our lives.

October 19 Our church was having a revival with Jack Taylor. We held a barbecue kick-off on the land we had just acquired for our new worship center. It was a wonderful time of food, fellowship and fun. As the evening came to an end a friend of ours came over to hug me and asked me what I had heard. I told him the usual "nothing new", then I heard myself say something else. "You know what? I know God has our little girl out there for me. I just know she is supposed to be here in time for Christmas to wear that red velvet dress! In a few more days that may not be a possibility; time is running out." He responded without missing a beat, "God is in control, Dana. He is capable of all kinds of miracles. Keep trusting Him to bring her home at *just* the right time." Something in his voice made me believe him.

October 23 9:30 a.m. The boys and I were having our daily devotional before we started school when the phone rang. I picked it up expecting to hear another person interested in OCC but instead I heard, "Dana, this is Charlotte. You have really been praying, haven't you?" My heart almost stopped beating. I managed to stutter a weak, "Yes, why?"

As calm as could be she replied, "We have a little girl for you." I think I remember dropping the phone and screaming. The boys looked at me wide-eyed but somehow immediately knew what was happening. "We're getting our sister!" they shouted, "We're getting our sister!"

The rest was a blur. Charlotte told me all she knew at that time was that our daughter was four months old from Changsha, China and that we would receive a Fed Ex package the following week with her picture and medical information. She also told us that even though there was a medical problem listed, there was a strong possibility that our daughter was perfectly healthy.

A baby! A real baby! I had dreamed and prayed for this phone call for so long, and it was finally here. The boys and I quickly cancelled school for the day, and we called Todd at the office. His secretary answered the phone and told me he was on another line.

The only thing I could think to say to her was, "Get him right now! We're having a baby!" I am pretty sure that got her attention because she dropped the phone, and we heard her running back to his office. When he came on the line we all started talking at one time but somehow managed to let him know that we had finally received our referral. There was a long silence on the other end of the line as we finished. We all waited to see what he was going to say. The man who had been so confident, so steadfast in his faith and so unwavering in his assurances for the past nine months only managed to say one word... "REALLY?"

I spent the next three or four hours calling every person we knew. It was an exciting day filled with great joy. That night we went to the final night of the revival at church. During the praise time all I could do was smile. I was so overwhelmed with a heart of gratefulness I could barely stand.

By the end of the evening everyone in the congregation knew our news, and there was a great spirit of rejoicing in that room. We even received our first baby gift that night, a miniature tea service from a special little friend of ours, Heidi.

Heidi was one remarkable child! She was five years old, and she was a true living miracle. She was born with a severe heart deformity, and the doctors gave her no chance to live. The doctors though didn't know Heidi's Mom and Dad, and they certainly didn't know the God they served! Through a series of miracles Heidi did survive. She was a healthy, happy girl. She was also my biggest prayer warrior. Heidi started praying for our daughter in June. She would pray every morning and every night without fail. Her Mom and Dad were amazed at how committed she was to praying for us.

Heidi and I became fast friends. She loved tea parties and often told me how my daughter and I would have tea parties together one day. So that night her gift was straight from the heart. We adults often think that children are too young to hear from God or too immature to know how to pray. All I know is that this little girl heard straight from the throne of God. He heard her precious prayers offered up on our behalf, every one of them. And I know that He was pleased. Heidi began praying the third week of June. The same week Netanya was born.

—⁂—

God, your Word says Your eyes are always on me. I choose to keep my focus on You. I will put my hope in You and rest in the knowledge that Your love for me in unfailing and eternal. I am not alone.

The God Who Provides for Us

Matthew 6:26

Look at the birds of the air; they do not sow or reap or store away in barns, and yet your Heavenly Father feeds them. Are you not much more valuable than they?

CHAPTER 11

October 29 The day we would see Netanya for the first time. The boys and I were so excited that we were dressed and ready for the day by 8:00 a.m. We spent the next two hours checking out the window every five minutes looking for the Fed Ex truck. Then at 10:10 a.m. we heard the familiar rumble of the truck. We all raced to the front porch.

The Fed Ex driver got out of her truck and stopped to look at us. She was probably just a little afraid, because there were the three of us hopping up and down on the front porch ready to pounce on her. As she walked slowly up the driveway eyeing us suspiciously I shouted to her, "We're having a baby, and you have her picture!" When she started backing up toward the truck I decided I better explain everything quickly before she jumped back in the truck and took off! Once she understood she congratulated us, and we raced inside with the package. We pulled out the paperwork and then... there she was. Netanya Jade Stone. Our third miracle baby. My rainbow.

She was incredible. The picture was in color, and she was wearing a cute little sun suit that said *Decked Out* in English on the front of it. She had amazing dark skin, beautiful dark eyes and a cute little button nose. I couldn't believe that I was finally looking at the daughter God created especially for our family. She looked exactly like the little girl in the dream I had many months earlier.

The boys were in awe. They had been praying every day for the last ten months for her, they had been down at the altar every Sunday with us, and now they were seeing the answer to all those prayers, right before their eyes.

Todd was in Oklahoma City on business that day. He told me to call him as soon as the picture came. In great detail I tried to describe her to him, and then I read him the medical report. She was born June 21, 1996. At three months when the picture was taken, she weighed eight pounds and was twenty-one inches long. According to the report *all her major organs were normal* and the last line read: *Conclusion: clubfooted.*

So that was the medical condition, a correctable medical condition. We were thrilled. The last information I gave Todd over the phone was her Chinese name, Liu Xi (Lou She). After I hung up I held her picture close to my heart for a while quietly thanking the Lord for creating her. I also gave thanks for the biological mother who gave birth to her. I knew she risked so much to make sure her daughter was given a chance to live. I will never fully understand the courage and strength it must have taken that mother to leave her daughter, knowing that she would never see her again. I just hoped that somehow she knew her daughter was now going to be in a loving home with a family that would provide everything she would ever need.

My next call was to a very special friend. We met Janice Meyer during the Worship/Ski Retreat. She may have been a stranger when we met her on the first day, but by the time we left she had captured our hearts. Janice worked for Life Outreach International, a ministry of James and Betty Robison, with headquarters not far from where we lived.

One of her main responsibilities was to travel to third world countries and through pictures tell the stories of the people living there. At the worship retreat she had shared her heart with us and told us all about the babies she had seen in different orphanages around the world. Todd and I wept as she described some of the living conditions. The common love we shared for the baby girls in China bonded us. Now she was going to be Netanya's godmother. I arranged to meet her at a camera shop, so we could enlarge the picture and make copies for all our family and friends. That afternoon I sent a copy to all our family, so they could finally put a face to Netanya Jade Stone, our daughter.

November 9 I began the day writing in my journal.

Journal entry:

As I read through your journal I see how many times God has had to strengthen my faith and trust; some lessons are so hard to learn! This waiting is excruciating. I look at your picture and wonder what you are doing, if you are crying, or sleeping, or hurting. It tears at my heart knowing that you could be in my arms right now; and yet I STAND on God's promise. He will be faithful to fulfill it soon!

I thought it had been difficult to wait for the referral to come. Now that we knew what she looked like it was actually even *more* difficult knowing that she was a real baby, *my* baby, in some faraway country out of my reach. I thought I would go crazy waiting for Gladney to give us updates over the next several weeks. Didn't they understand that Christmas was coming? That red velvet dress was hanging in her closet ready for the Christmas Eve service at our church. What was the delay?

But of course they had to be very cautious. No time frames, no sure answers just patience required by all. And Charlotte kept reminding us that until we got our final approval from Beijing it wasn't a done deal.

Thankfully Operation Christmas Child was upon us. We were having the shoebox dedication service that Sunday and the next two weeks would be spent running the Collection Center. That meant being at the church daily to make sure things were running smoothly. I've heard that if you reach out to help someone else you will get a new perspective on your problems or worries and that was definitely true in my case. I was having such a great time meeting all the people bringing in their shoeboxes that time seemed to fly by. The testimonies from people and their excitement for the ministry were a wonderful faith builder for me. It was a reminder of how important each of us is in the Lord's eyes and how we need to share His message of hope, healing and life. I knew that if God used people like this to bring joy into the lives of little children around the world, He would certainly be using someone to take love and take care of my Netanya.

November 24 The forecast called for ice, sleet and snow and it was starting to do all three. This was the day that all of the shoeboxes needed to be loaded up and taken over to the regional center in Dallas. It was also the day our church friends were hosting a baby shower for us. After church we finished getting all the shoeboxes into cartons and began loading them into box trucks. I had set a goal of 2,000 shoeboxes, but by the end of the day we had a final count of 4,000 shoeboxes!

Once the boxes were loaded we turned our attention to enjoying the baby shower honoring Netanya. Our home group prepared the room beautifully and made sure there were lots of Noah's arks and rainbows everywhere. We were surprised at how many of our friends braved the inclement weather to celebrate with us. Halfway through opening all the gifts, Todd asked, "Are we going to get anything besides pink?" A chorus of "No way!" filled the room! One thing was certain; Netanya was going to be a very well dressed little girl. After the party, we got into the trucks and drove to Dallas to deliver all the shoeboxes. As the snow began to fall we basked in the love and encouragement of our friends. It was a wonderful, wonderful day.

November 26 Thanksgiving was two days away. All of my family was coming to celebrate with us, and I was scurrying around cooking up a storm. That afternoon I got a phone call from a woman who had adopted a baby from China through Gladney. She was interested in adopting a second child, which would make her "SN" (special needs) so she was watching our case closely. I met her at some of the Gladney functions, but I didn't really know why she was calling me. The way she started the conversation confused and upset me, "How are you? Are you just devastated? I've wanted to call you for several days, but I was so upset that I didn't know what to say to make you feel better."

I couldn't imagine what she was talking about, so I just said, "Well, everything's fine, why?" What she said next sent a shockwave through my body. "You must be just crushed. I went to Gladney a few days ago, and they told me that all the other families who received referrals were going to travel next month except you."

It took everything in me to utter another word. I quickly told her I hadn't heard that and that I needed to go. I sank down to the floor and thought to myself, "Not again. I can't do this again." It took me over two hours to reach Charlotte, but she reassured me that everything was okay. The information I had received over the phone was correct, but thankfully, it was also skewed. There were a total of twelve families who had received referrals. Six of those families were not considered special needs. They had been given a travel date of December 14 to go to China.

The other six families, of which we were included, were all considered SN. She told me that the Chinese government had a problem finalizing a definitive definition of what special needs would be and they were in the process of making a list of all medical conditions that would designate the SN category. Until that list came out Gladney had been told that we needed to wait to make sure our daughter's medical condition was on the new list before we traveled.

So the waiting game continued. They had finally approved us to adopt our daughter, but now they would not let us get her. I just couldn't believe it. I went into my bedroom and picked up the one thing that could steady my mind and my heart, my Bible. As I read John 15:4-8 He reminded me anew of the importance of being totally dependent on Him.

> "Remain in me, and I will remain in you. No branch can bear fruit by itself; it must remain in the vine . . . If you remain in me and my words remain in you, ask whatever you wish, and it will be given to you."

He had given me His word, His promise. He had also given me the Sword in Isaiah 55 with which to battle the enemy. Now my assignment was to remain steadfast in Him and trust in His plan and His path to our daughter. I could do that! My heart immediately filled with peace, and I headed back into the kitchen to prepare for our feast.

Thanksgiving was a joyful time in our home. We put Netanya's picture on the table so that she could join us in spirit as we celebrated. She may not have been there in the physical sense yet but she was certainly there in our hearts. As we went around the table that day giving testimony to all of God's blessings, Netanya was on the top of everyone's list.

God, your Word says that I am valuable to You, and as Your child You will provide for me. I choose to focus on all the ways You take care of my needs instead of worrying about what I want. I will have a heart of gratitude and praise You for all that You do for me each day. I am not alone.

The God Who We Can Trust

Proverbs 3:5-6

Trust in the Lord with all your heart and lean not on your own understanding; acknowledge Him in all your ways and He will make straight your path.

CHAPTER 12

December 3 Time was running out and I felt it. I sat down to write in Netanya's journal and share my heart.

Journal entry:

So many feelings and thoughts are constantly running through my head. When will our phone ever ring with the news of our travel date? How am I going to make it through each day until then? Yet above it all I know that God is and will be faithful. He gives me sign after sign of His promise to bring you home to us. I just need to stay in that outpouring of grace that He pours over me each and every day.

God knew my heart. He knew that I sometimes struggled, and yet in His mercy He kept bringing me comfort, strength and peace through His Word and through people that He brought into our lives on a daily basis. He kept reminding me that I wasn't on this journey by myself. He was with me every step of the way.

We had recently been given two Scriptures. The first was from Isaiah 66:9, "...do I bring to the moment of birth and not give delivery, says the Lord?" The second Scripture was also from Isaiah 8:17-18, "I will wait for the Lord; I will put my trust in Him. Here am I, and the children the Lord has given me." The Scriptures were declarations to me; reminders that I needed to wait for my situation to line up with His Word. He continually reassured me not to listen to what the world may be saying about the delay but instead look up, listen and trust Him alone.

That afternoon the boys and I went to the mall to do some Christmas shopping. As we walked past the ladies department of a local store, a shirt hanging on the wall by itself caught my attention. It was a pretty dark green sweatshirt and on the front was a Noah's Ark with a rainbow above it. I went over to read what was underneath the ark and couldn't believe it when I read, "When in doubt... remember the promise of the rainbow." Of course, I had to have that shirt! When I took it to the checkout counter the woman behind the counter looked at it and said, "That's strange, I have never seen this shirt before." I just smiled and told her that it was made just for me! I wore that shirt a lot in the next few months. It was a tangible reminder of how God sometimes uses great imagination and creativity to reassure His children.

December 9 It was time for a reality check. There would be no last minute reprieve for us. The six couples would be going to China without us. I knew I could trust in God's timing, but my mind was trying to figure out why God would put that vision of Netanya in her red velvet dress for Christmas in my heart if He wasn't going to fulfill it. There had to be a reasonable explanation for it, but that movie frame was simply not making any sense to me right now.

I woke up in a bad mood that day and the mood continued all day. I couldn't believe how often I had to battle with my emotions during those days. That particular day, I was losing the battle. By the time I got ready to go to our annual Women's Christmas party that evening I was downright grumpy. I really wanted to be on that plane on the 14th with the other families, yet here I was, still home while they were packing bags and preparing to travel. I knew I needed to go the party because my friends would all be there, and if anyone could get my mind off of China they could! The evening would be a lot of fun with a dinner and an ornament exchange. The highlight of the evening would be my friend Vickie, Heidi's mom, sharing her testimony of Miracle Heidi. Although I was not really in the mood to be festive, something inside me said to get up and go.

As I grudgingly drove to the party, I muttered to God the whole way. As I got out of the car I actually challenged Him and said, "Okay God, if you are really in control of this adoption could you at least give me a sign? How about letting me get an ornament that will let me know that you are still working on this for me?" I went inside and made it through dinner and fellowship, waiting to see if God would answer my challenge. Heidi came running over and sat on my lap to help as we played a game of musical chairs for the ornament exchange. Every time the music stopped I wondered if the ornament in my hands was *the one*. After exchanging the ornaments several times they finally told us to open our gift bags. Inside my bag was a little teddy bear inside a stocking. Heidi loved it, but me? I pouted.

All I could think was, "Great, I can't even get a simple ornament to make me feel better!" Heidi begged me for the teddy ornament, and I quickly handed it over to her. "I don't want a dumb old bear anyway," I thought to myself. As those thoughts rumbled around in my head I looked up to see Vickie standing in front of me. With big tears in her eyes she said, "Dana, I have the wrong ornament. God said these are for you!"

She handed me a small box, and I opened it up to find two handmade Chinese dolls in beautiful silk outfits. God instantly spoke to my heart and said,

"Dana, I heard your cry. I know you are hurting. I know you are tired of waiting. I have told you again and again, I am here. I am answering your cry tonight like you asked, but I want you to notice that I did not give them directly to you. Do you trust Me? Do you REALLY trust Me? I have never left your side through this journey... not ONE time have I turned away, and I *will* give you the desire of your heart."

I silently and tearfully asked the Lord to forgive me, *again*.

As Vickie begin to share her testimony Heidi got a little antsy, so we got up to go exploring for a few minutes. We spent a few minutes looking at the beautiful Christmas decorations and then went into an adjoining room to talk. We had been sitting there a few minutes when I heard Vickie say something about December 14. My ears instantly perked up, and I told Heidi I wanted to hear what her mommy was saying so we hurried back into the kitchen to listen. Vickie was sharing about an incident that happened while Heidi was still in the hospital, critically ill. God had given Vickie a word at the beginning of their ordeal that Heidi would be healed and that she would grow up happy and healthy. She clung to that word daily waiting for the circumstances to line up with His word. But they didn't seem to be doing that in the natural realm. And then she shared this part of her story:

She was going to the hospital at the beginning of December when she noticed a marquee on a local theater that said, "On Stage--Heidi December 14-22." Vickie said she just *knew* that it was a sign from God. He was going to heal Heidi on the 14th and she would go home on the 22nd in time for Christmas. She was so excited and looked forward with great anticipation to the 14th.

But on the 14th Heidi got worse. Vickie couldn't understand why God would do such a thing. In that moment Vickie's faith was tested. Over the next few days, Heidi would improve and then regress, causing much concern. But on December 22nd she came off the respirator for the first time in her life.

What had God showed her through this? That she had taken His word, His promise to heal Heidi and added her *own* interpretation to it. She had seen that marquee and decided that it had to be a sign from God. That decision led to a difficult lesson where she learned that she needed to stand on God's word but *not exaggerate it*. She was reminded to be confident in His word and be patient and content to wait for His timing to bring that word to fruition.

In that moment I knew exactly why I was there that night. I needed to hear Vickie's December 14th story and the date was certainly no coincidence. It was straight from the loving heart of God. I finally understood why I had been on such an emotional roller coaster over the last two months. I had put *my* time frame on God's promise. I had taken His promise of bringing Netanya into our lives and exaggerated it. God had not given me an exact date or time for bringing our daughter home, *I had*. I learned at the end of the evening that right before I came into the room to hear her story Vickie stopped and said, "Well, I've never shared *this* part of my testimony before but the Holy Spirit wants someone here tonight to hear my December 14th story." What a sweet reminder it was to me that God cares about every detail in our lives and that His ear is always turned toward us and His eye never wanders from us.

As I was preparing to leave the party I was telling someone about what God had done that evening when a friend named Helen came up behind me. Helen's daughter Carolyn was a missionary in China. Helen said, "Oh, you got my little ornaments! You know, I was wondering who they were for. I went to get an ornament a few days ago, and I found a really cute one. But when I went to pay for it, God told me to put it back up and get those Chinese dolls instead. I didn't think they were very cute but God told me twice to go get them."

As I drove home that night I felt the overwhelming presence of a loving and devoted God. My whole attitude had changed in a few short hours. I was thankful for people who were so in tune with the Spirit and so willing to follow His prompting. The Lord had taught me many things that night and finally the roller coaster of emotions was brought into line with His promise. I would be so very thankful for that revelation in the weeks to come.

—⚬—

God, your Word says that You will make my path straight when I learn to trust in You. I choose to put my trust in Your plan and not rush ahead. I will lean into You and acknowledge Your authority in my life. I am not alone.

The God Who Gives Us Rest

Psalm 62:1-2

*Truly my soul finds rest in God; my salvation comes from him.
Truly He is my rock and my salvation;
He is my fortress, I will never be shaken.*

CHAPTER 13

December 15 *"Some trust in chariots and some in horses, but we trust in the name of the Lord our God".* I spent the day before repeating that verse over and over again. Six families had boarded a plane yesterday bound for China and their daughters. Their return date was December 25, Christmas Day. Finally, I was truly able to rejoice for all of them. This would be an incredibly special Christmas for those families. They would experience the joy of becoming a parent for the first time. It would be something they would remember for the rest of their lives.

As I sat in Sunday school that day I was able to release the vision I had held onto of that Christmas Eve Service with my daughter in her red velvet dress. I felt renewed hope and a stronger trust in His vision than I had ever felt. I knew that His plan and His purpose would be fulfilled in our lives. A lot of prayers were offered up that morning for us. Our friends knew we had hoped to have Netanya home for Christmas.

As they gathered around us at the end of class to pray, a good friend told me she saw a vision of Netanya sleeping in her crib with a bright light totally surrounding her. She said the light was the presence of the Lord keeping her safe and protected. I cherished that picture in my mind. It brought me immense peace knowing that the Creator of the entire universe had His eye on my daughter and His hand of protection was hovering over her.

Our church service was wonderful that morning. The message Dean shared touched me deeply and brought even more peace to my heart. He talked about people who were in need of a miracle and the importance of believing that the miracle would occur. He had a big sign on the podium that said, *Expect a Miracle*. By the end of the day that sign was hanging on my bathroom mirror.

December 24 Christmas Eve. Todd's parents, his sister and her family were all with us for Christmas. As we prepared for Christmas Eve service I was determined to enjoy this holy celebration of God's greatest gift to man, the birth of His Son Jesus Christ. I knew that going to church that night would be a little difficult. I knew it might stir up some sadness, and I needed to be prepared. That night there seemed to be babies everywhere, and the first baby I saw as I entered the sanctuary was a little girl in a red velvet dress. The enemy had landed a direct hit yet once again, my church family was there for us. One after another friends kept coming up to us offering hugs and prayers.

As we went to the altar for communion and knelt with open hearts before the Lord, we soon felt the soft warm hands that had held ours so often through this journey, the hands of our pastor. He had stopped serving communion and had come to pray with us. The presence of the Lord was so sweetly evident in that moment, and we quietly basked in it. When we stood to leave we knew that the enemy's best shot had been cast aside by the power and majesty of our Heavenly Father.

Christmas was wonderful, and we had so much fun with all the family. The Stone's brought Netanya her first doll, and my mom had the beautiful Noah's Ark stocking complete with a rainbow. When we hung the stocking beside the others we decided to leave it up until the day we brought Netanya home.

That evening we turned on the local news to see a report from the airport about the couples coming home from China with their brand new daughters. We were completely mesmerized by the beaming parents and their precious little girls. I knew that soon it would be us. Something else welled up within my spirit in that moment. It bubbled up from deep within me, and at that very moment the Lord spoke so clearly to me. He told me that our moment... THE moment was coming... and coming very soon.

---

*God, your Word says that You are my rock and my fortress.
I choose to run to You when life is hard, and I am weak.
I will rest within Your strong arms and allow You to
bring peace to my weary soul. I am not alone.*

The God Who Brings Exceeding Joy

Acts 2:28

You have made known to me paths of life; You will fill me with joy in Your presence.

CHAPTER 14

December 30 The phone rang and it was Charlotte. My heart stopped when she uttered the words I had waited so long to hear; "Your final approval just came through. Are you ready to go to China?" She was so excited as she told me that the orphanage in Changsha had given their final approval to us as well as the other five families. All that was left to do was collect all the paperwork, and our travel date would be set!

Mr. George Wu, a Gladney staff representative, was working day and night trying to keep us updated on all the latest information. He had been working tirelessly for us over the last few months and all of his hard work was finally paying off. Charlotte told me to go ahead and block off the last two weeks in January. As I hung up the phone my knees buckled, and I slipped to the ground and quietly gave thanks to God for His faithfulness and love. We were so close!

December 31 Midnight. Todd was fast asleep, but I wanted to stay up and welcome in the year that would finally bring our daughter home. I sat up thanking the Lord for being in every moment of this journey, for never leaving our side and for creating our beautiful Netanya. It was a special time in the presence of the Lord. I couldn't think of a better way to start the New Year.

January 2 The phone call finally came. The paperwork was complete, the appointments were arranged and we were on our way to China! "You need to be in Hong Kong on January 25th," Charlotte said. I hung up the phone and immediately called Todd. We began to discuss flight options, and Todd decided to arrange our flight schedule as soon as possible. He spent the day arranging our trip, and a few days later we were really glad he did because we learned that our trip coincided with the Chinese New Year, and all flights in and out of China were booked solid. We heard that several of the couples that were in our travel group had more than a few tense moments as they tried to find an available flight. Once again, we were thankful for the Lord prompting us to action.

January 3 I had hardly slept a wink the night before. All I could do was lay there thinking about having my daughter placed in my arms for the first time. I wondered what she would look like now, after three months of growing. I wondered what she smelled like and what her little fingers would feel like wrapped around mine. The 25th seemed an eternity away, but in the meantime we had a lot to do! Staying true to the organizational geek within me I made a list that morning of all the basics we would need. We asked Charlotte to send us a copy of the addresses and phone numbers of the other five couples that would travel with us, so we could introduce ourselves and compare packing lists.

The process of adopting internationally was unlike anything most people could understand. In many ways we had put our whole lives on hold over the last fifteen months. It was like living in a vacuum. Friends would try to tell me it was just like being pregnant, but every time someone would say that to me I would just think, *I don't think so!* At least when you are pregnant, your baby is with you all the time. You can feel it growing, moving and kicking and you know within about a two-week window exactly when that baby will be in your arms. You can get excited as the months grow short (or long, depending on how you feel that day!), as you prepare the baby room, have baby showers and plan for your life together.

International adoption meant that you were at the mercy of a foreign government that could change direction at a moment's notice and had no compulsion to offer you a time frame. You couldn't plan ahead; all you could do was wait on someone else to tell you if and when you could bring your child home!

The next day one of couples that would travel with us came over, and we had a wonderful time getting to know each other. Bill and Gloria had an eight-year-old adopted daughter named Rebecca. Their referral from China was for an eight-month-old little girl who they had named Kimberly. Her medical condition was officially stated as "cross-eyed," although she sure didn't look it in her picture. She was a beautiful child with lots of hair.

Over the next few weeks we spent a lot of time on the phone helping each other prepare for every imaginable situation that might arise. We knew we would be in another country, not just down the street. We wouldn't have a convenience store to go to if we ran out or forgot something. We had to have everything we might possibly need. It was challenging to say the least, but we had so much fun preparing!

When we went to church on Sunday there was yet another wonderful time of celebration. Thunderous applause greeted us as our praise report was read to the congregation. We had called Pastor Dean earlier in the week to tell him the news, and as the service started he came down into our pew with a huge grin on his face and said, "Expect a miracle? We just got one!" As he embraced us we felt the love of the Father envelope us. I knew God was as excited as we were that one of His little ones was finally coming home to the *forever family* she had been destined for from the very beginning.

January 6 Charlotte had given me the name of one of the couples who came home Christmas Day from China, so we could contact them for some helpful hints in our travel planning. I called them at their home in Virginia and left a message on their recorder. They returned my phone call the next day, but not from their home in Virginia. They just happened to be in Texas visiting family and were only twenty minutes from where we lived. They volunteered to come over and give us any help they could.

We invited them for dinner, along with Bill and Gloria. We were armed with a list of questions and grilled them throughout the evening. They brought their new seven-month-old daughter with them. She was so precious, and I watched her all night just dreaming about the time very soon when I would hold my daughter in my arms. It was a wonderful evening, and they were so gracious to give up a night for us. We learned valuable insights and added lots more to our "to get" lists. Those lists were growing larger and larger all the time!

January 9 With all the hectic preparation going on around our home I wanted to slow my mind down for a few minutes and penned my thoughts,

Journal entry:

"Time seems to be passing so slowly right now and yet at the same time very quickly! It has been such a hectic time of preparing for you, but a time of joy, laughter and celebration. My heart simply leaps for joy every time I walk by your room. It is ready for you now, and I can't wait till the day I walk by that room and know that you are finally home where you belong. I sit and look at your picture so often, trying to imprint it on my mind and heart. I know you will look different when we see you for the first time, but I know I will recognize you instantly. Netanya, the Spirit of the Lord is on you. It shows in your eyes. Through them really! We have been praying specifically that you would hear our voices in your sleep and see our faces in your dreams so that you will recognize us too! God has been so faithful. He has given us our heart's desire, fulfilling

His promise. You will be a living example of God's miraculous hand of power and might, grace and mercy. What a testimony you will be."

January 11 We received a huge packet of information from Gladney with helpful hints as well as a list of things we would need for the trip. The items that were causing the most stress were the gifts that we needed for the officials in China. It was customary to give each official and each guide as well as bus drivers and other helpers small gifts of appreciation for their services. We were told we would need twelve to fourteen gifts some for men, some for women and some that could be for either. Gladney had given us a list of good suggestions, but I wanted to make sure we had enough and that each gift would be especially nice. There were so many things to try to remember and prepare for, and I was starting to feel the pressure!

January 14 Life was one big hustle now. We spent most of our waking hours preparing for the trip. It was all so very exciting, and the boys had a great time picking out outfits for their sister. She was going to be so blessed to have two such wonderful, loving big brothers. Someone had asked me a few days earlier how Joshua and Jacob were handling all the uproar around Netanya and if they were a little jealous of her. I told Joshua later on that day about the conversation, and he responded indignantly, "Mom! They have got to be kidding. Don't they know how hard we have prayed for her too?"

A reporter from the local newspaper came out to do an interview with us for a feature article she was writing about our adoption story. She was very engaging and gave us a wonderful opportunity to share about not only our journey to our daughter but also about our ever-faithful God. She had so many questions she ended up staying for almost two hours. The article appeared in the newspaper several days later, and we were thrilled at the response we received from our community. It seemed that everyone in our town was buzzing about welcoming two beautiful little girls from China to their new homes!

That night we went to a meeting at church. Todd and I sat through the whole meeting in a daze and when someone ended up having to ask us the same question several times before we responded everyone just laughed and said, "Don't ask them anything. They're going to China." It was true. We walked around with big, silly grins on our faces all the time.

Only eight days to go.

God, your Word says that when I am in Your presence, You will fill me with joy. I choose to spend time each day with You so that Your joy will find a home in my heart. I am not alone.

THE GOD WHO HEARS OUR PRAYERS

I Peter 3:12

For the eyes of the Lord are on the righteous and His ears are attentive to their prayer.

CHAPTER 15

January 17

Journal entry:

"Time is speeding up and there is so much to do in these last couple of days. I am starting to get a little more anxious. Will you like us? Will we have the right essentials for you? How about formula? How many diapers? What kind of pacifiers and bottles will you like? I want everything to be perfect for you. I want you to feel loved and protected from the moment we see you. I want you to know that you will never be lonely again; or cry without someone being there for you. I want you to know that there will always be a shoulder for you to rest on and arms ready to carry you. How special you are. Before I even see or touch your face I couldn't love you more. And as much as I already love you, your Heavenly Father adores you more than I ever could."

That night as I prayed with the boys their prayers absolutely amazed me. They had become such incredible prayer warriors for Netanya and their prayers were mature beyond their young years. Jacob prayed that God would "remove any mountains that were between Netanya and us" and reminded the enemy that he "couldn't keep those mountains up when Jesus was around."

Joshua's prayer started like this, "I speak to the enemy and tell you to flee in Jesus' name, and any attacks from the enemy that you are using to try to block this adoption will fail because of Jesus' blood." He also prayed for all the other babies in our group and their families, as well as all the babies in the orphanages, that they would know how much Jesus loved them. Their prayers were so powerful and so anointed, and I knew they were going straight to the throne of God.

Each night after the boys went to bed I would get on the Internet to do more research. It was an incredible source of information as we prepared for our trip. One of the really cool sites I found was an online community message board set up for families waiting for referrals as well as those getting ready to travel. Families who had already adopted would give information and helpful hints as well as detailed lists of things to take, not to take, etc. We visited those sites each day to ensure that we were as knowledgeable as possible. We learned quickly that this group of people connected by a common thread of adoption was a real family. Everyone was supportive to those who were discouraged, encouraged those needing help, and rejoiced with those who received referrals and traveled to bring their child home.

We also noticed that a lot of them were Christians, and we were surprised and blessed to see that their faith had played an important role in our adoption process. A prayer session had been set up online New Year's Eve. Everyone was encouraged to send in their prayers to the site and from 11 p.m. New Year's Eve until 2:00 a.m. they prayed for all the requests. One area they specifically focused a large amount of prayer on was all those waiting for referrals and travel approval.

They prayed fervently that those referrals and approvals would start flooding out across the nation beginning the next day, January 2. We received our travel approval on January 2nd. James 5:16 states, "The faithful prayers of a righteous man availeth much." We were so thankful for the fervent prayers of hundreds of people we would never meet who took the time to reach out to the Father on our behalf. I firmly believe those prayers were answered right on time!

January 18 Today I would finally get to pack my daughter's suitcase. We had so much fun placing each and every item carefully inside. I couldn't believe the time had finally come and that in just a few days we would board a plane to China. In the mail that day I received a letter from a prayer partner friend of mine. She seemed to always know when I needed prayer or encouragement, and she was quick to respond to the Spirit's prompting. Her letter gave me a sweet sense of peace and confidence in the midst of the busyness around me. It was yet another reminder that the Lord had been and would be with us every step of the way.

She wrote that as the Israelites were preparing to go into the Promised Land, they were fearful of the inhabitants, but the Lord reassured them that He would go ahead of them and make a way. He reminded them of all He had done to bring them out of Egypt and all that He had done to get them to this point.

She felt led to remind us that we were much like the Israelites. We were getting ready to go into a new land; a land God had promised us we would enter and He wanted us to know He had already gone ahead of us to prepare the way. She shared that we were not to fear the unknown but that we were simply to remember God's faithfulness through it all and that we were to stand firm, trust Him and go into the land with His peace. It was exactly what I had needed to hear. My joy and excitement grew as I released every aspect of our trip to Him.

That night after everyone had gone to bed I went into Netanya's room and sat in her rocking chair to sing her song. As I sat there I realized with all the hustle and bustle of the last few weeks I had not spent much time with the Lord, so that night I did. It was a wonderfully sweet time and before I went to bed I prayed this prayer,

"Here I am Lord, seeking you, praising you, and lifting Netanya up to you in prayer. I want to stand in the gap for her tonight, Lord. I want to pray once again for her health, her protection, and her peace. Watch over her, Lord, keep Your hand on her, place Your angels around her. Speak to her spirit, let her see our faces, and hear our voices in her dreams. Hold her tight, Father. You promised you would, and I trust completely in You."

January 20 The last Sunday we would walk into church without our daughter in our arms. We asked a few of our friends to gather around us and pray for us, and as we knelt at the altar we sensed many had come. Our children's pastor prayed and his prayer touched on every emotion we had experienced, our fear and anxiety, our hope and desires. The presence of the Lord was palpable at that moment, and we knew He was right there in that circle with us. It was one of the sweetest moments of our journey and everyone that was gathered around lingered as long as possible, soaking in His presence.

January 21 12:30 a.m. in the morning, and we were still packing! Our biggest problem at the moment was that once we had finished packing all the suitcases, we found that not only was there a restriction on the number of suitcases allowed, there was also a strict size and weight requirement on each piece. I spent most of the day repacking and trying to hunt down specific sizes of suitcases from friends. By the time we had everything rounded up and repacked Netanya's suitcase was so full that the boys and I had to sit on it to get it closed!

As the days grew closer and closer to our departure it was becoming more difficult preparing to leave the boys. As a family we didn't like being away from each other, and this was going to be very tough on all of us. The day we were scheduled to leave was also Jacob's sixth birthday. I dreaded leaving him on such a special day. The airport goodbyes the next day would be difficult, but it was a reminder to me that our children are not really ours after all. The

Lord had blessed us with beautiful gifts, ones that we were to cherish every day and trust that the Lord had them in the palm of His hand even when we weren't with them.

We tried not to talk about the fact that we would be separated for two weeks. We chose to focus on thinking about all the fun they were going to have at Grandma's house, including the fun of having a swimming pool and hot tub in her back yard. The boys would also be able to spend time with my sister, her husband and their four children who lived across the street from my mom. My brother and his wife had also arranged to take the boys for a few days. I knew the boys would be very busy, and they would have plenty of love and attention lavished on them.

January 22 We spent the day getting the boys' bags packed and having fun together as a family. Jacob came up to me at one point and said, "I don't want Daddy to pray for us, because it will make me cry." We have a tradition in our family that when one of us goes on a trip the rest of the family gathers together and prays over that person. It is important to all of us to ask for the Lord's protection and peace on the person traveling away from home and this trip would be no different. So that evening as we prepared to take them to the airport I told Todd what Jacob had said. He brought the boys into the living room and said, "Okay, we know we are all going to cry so we might as well do it in the comfort of our own home!" We sat down together on the couch and did just that. It was a tough couple of minutes, but it also released the tension that had been building. After a wonderful and sweet time of prayer, we packed up the car and headed out to the airport. I said my goodbyes on the jet way ramp, and Todd took the boys onto the plane to make sure they were comfortable. When he came back off the plane we walked out to the car in silence and both had a good cry!

We got home around 8:30 that night with a lot of work ahead of us. Our plane left at 7:30 a.m. the next morning, so we got busy. We were knee deep in clothes and diapers when the doorbell rang. I opened the door to find our pastor with another couple from our church. They had come over to see us one more time before we left and wanted to pray for us. We spent about an hour just visiting and praying. It meant so much to us that they had come and were truly thankful for the prayers.

When they left, Todd worked on our laptop testing it to make sure it worked properly. We were going to use email to keep all of our friends updated throughout our trip so they would know exactly what was happening and how to pray.

We finished packing around 1:30 a.m., and I crawled into bed too excited to sleep. Todd stayed up a few more hours finishing up office work before he collapsed into bed beside me. We couldn't believe that in a short time we would finally be on our way to China. The final part of our journey was about to begin.

God, your Word says You hear my prayers. I choose to invite You into every area of my life and I will be intentional in including You as I seek direction in decisions I will make, both big and small. I am not alone.

The God Who Is Faithful

Psalm 33:4

For the word of the Lord is right and true;
He is faithful in all He does.

CHAPTER 16

January 23 5:00 a.m. We stumbled out of bed trying to grasp the fact that the day had finally arrived. We gathered our luggage, got dressed and prepared to leave for the airport. Before we left I went into Netanya's room one last time. The crib now empty would soon hold a beautiful little girl. The changing table quiet now would soon be the place of cooing and giggling. The rocking chair silent and still would soon be a place of warm embrace for me to sing songs of love to my daughter as she slipped off to sleep each night. This room that had been put together so lovingly would finally be filled with the sounds and smells of Netanya Jade Stone. Tears filled my eyes, and I stood in the middle of the room and declared, "Soon Netanya, soon." Our neighbor drove us out to the airport and dropped us off at the terminal. We checked our luggage and made our way to the gate and after what seemed like hours, it was finally time to board the plane.

The flight to San Francisco was uneventful. Both of us caught a few winks of sleep before we landed. We had a two-hour delay before we were able to board our plane bound for Hong Kong. We ate lunch while we waited and tried not to get too anxious, and as we boarded our flight to Hong Kong I remarked to Todd that the next time we entered the United States we would be a family of five. It brought a huge smile to his face!

Flying time to Hong Kong was fifteen hours, but it felt like *forever*! Our trip to Israel had been a little over eleven hours, and it hadn't really seemed that long. This trip however, seemed like an eternity. The first few hours we spent talking and taking a nap. The next twelve hours were spent trying not to go stir crazy. There were three movies, numerous short films, lots of food and increasingly numb backsides.

Journal entry:

Wow, only a little over halfway there. This has been the longest flight EVER! Every inch of my body is screaming. I just want to get there and get closer to where you are. It seems like time is slowing down to a snail's pace. If I am this impatient now, it's going to be a long two days!

When Todd woke from one of his naps, he said, "Good grief, I am tired of sitting here. How much longer is the flight?" I chuckled and said, "Oh, only about another seven hours." Not really the answer he was looking for, but both of us knew this part of the journey was important and that patience was required. The end result would be so worth the wait. Labor had begun.

January 24 9:30 p.m., Hong Kong time. We arrived! I had never been happier to walk on solid ground in all our lives. Our legs felt like noodles by the time we stepped off that plane, and our bodies thought it was 7:30 a.m. We had been up for over twenty-four hours and had magically lost fourteen hours of our day. We retrieved our five very large pieces of luggage and made our way toward customs. While Todd went to commandeer a luggage cart I tried to clear the cobwebs from my brain. Thankfully, we breezed through customs and without even a look they waved us through. It appeared that the guards were very accustomed to Americans arriving loaded to the gills with luggage and baby equipment. We made our way outside to find a cab and tried to communicate our desired destination to the driver. This proved to be quite a challenge. We handed him a preprinted card that Gladney had given us with the hotel name and address and a small map all in Chinese. You would have thought it was in Portuguese by the response we got from our driver! He had no clue where the hotel was or what the card said. Finally, after five or six minutes of trying to communicate with him, a man in a long white coat came over and stepped in to assist us, and we were soon on our way to the Salisbury Hotel in downtown Hong Kong. We sat in the back seat praying silently that the driver truly did know where he was going! We made it to our hotel a short ten minutes later and learned our first lesson about taxis in Hong Kong. They automatically add a tip to the cab fare. When the driver gave Todd the amount due we kept trying to give him more as a tip. We had that poor driver totally confused by the time he left. He couldn't figure out why those crazy Americans kept trying to shove more money at him!

We entered the hotel and found it to be very nice. As Todd checked in at the main desk I sat down to catch my breath. I looked around and realized for the first time that we were half a world away from our home, in a different country, on a different continent and definitely in the minority. It was somewhat surreal. I began to feel a little anxious and fearful. What if she doesn't like me? What if something goes wrong now? What if we don't have all the right paperwork? My mind was physically and mentally tired, and as I sat there trying to calm my nerves I suddenly noticed a song that was playing over the speakers in the lobby. The song was the classic hymn, "Great Is Thy Faithfulness."

I had to smile at the thought that here we were in a Communist country and yet this beautiful hymn was playing. It instantly made me feel at home and at peace. The words began to penetrate my spirit and as the third verse played, it brought restored clarity and confidence. God is faithful. He alone had brought us to this point, and He alone was going to bring us to the end of our journey and in that I could be assured.

After Todd finished checking us in we took the elevator to our room. We were both ready to fall into a nice big bed and get some much-needed rest. Of course that meant we needed to actually get *into* our room, which turned into quite the comedy. The locking systems for rooms in that hotel were very different than what we were accustomed to, and it took us over ten minutes to figure out how to open our door. Once we finally got in we realized our dreams of falling into a nice soft bed were just that- a dream.

What we found were two small twin beds that were rock hard, but we were just too tired to care. All I wanted was a hot shower and sleep. Unfortunately, that ended up not going any better than getting our key to work in the door. We couldn't get any of the light switches to turn on! We spent the next twenty minutes in the dark, totally frustrated and trying everything we could to find the master switch. Then from somewhere in the deep recesses of my exhausted mind I remembered reading something on the web about your room key activating all the electricity in the room. Behind the door I found the magic panel. I inserted the room key and voila! every electric apparatus in the room turned on, full blast. T.V., radio, lights blared as we scurried around trying to deaden the noise before we woke up everyone around us.

Exhausted beyond belief by this point Todd began to unpack our bag, while I grabbed a shower and washed my hair. I came out of the bathroom feeling refreshed and ready for bed, but first I needed to dry my hair. This ensued my *third* lesson about hotels in China. I plugged the hair dryer into the electrical adaptor we had gotten for the trip, but when I turned the dryer on I immediately blew the fuse for the entire room. Todd just looked at me and started to laugh… thank goodness! I had inadvertently put the adaptor on the wrong voltage and had managed to fry the fuse AND my hair dryer. We called down to the front desk and tried to explain what had happened. Someone from housekeeping came up and Todd finally managed to get the young man to understand our dilemma. After a half hour wait we had a new fuse and were back in business. I fell into bed with wet hair, and we were both asleep in less than five minutes.

January 25 We slept in and had breakfast in the hotel restaurant. As we prayed over our meal another beautiful hymn filled the room over the speakers. It was a beautiful way to start our first full day in China. After breakfast we went to meet up with our friend, Carolyn. She was the daughter of the woman who gave me the Chinese Christmas ornaments in December. Carolyn was a missionary in China and had been living there for four years. She was so excited to have someone visit her, and it gave us the chance to catch her up on all the latest news from home. We had a wonderful time together seeing different sites around Hong Kong. It was a fun day, and we got to experience just about every form of transportation as we explored the city. By the end of the day we had ridden in a taxi, bus, subway, tram, boat and train. We were exhausted but were glad that we had a day to adjust to the time change and relax before our time was not our own. As we crawled into bed that night we were excited to know that we were one day closer to our daughter!

January 26 That morning Carolyn took us to her church. Religious restrictions were more relaxed in Hong Kong, because they were not under Chinese rule yet. We had such a wonderful time worshipping with the locals, and it was really fun to see that there were people all over the world who believe, worship and adore the same God we do. After church we walked down to a local street market. What a learning experience that was! The cultural differences are vast when it comes to food selection and none were more apparent than their choices of protein. Suffice it to say that I chose to walk by the meat section quickly and didn't look in any of the containers!

When we were done she took me back to the hotel to finish packing. Todd went with her to buy pearl necklaces for our moms.

He also purchased a round jade stone with a red fabric chain for Netanya. We were told that it was customary in China for new parents to place a necklace like this around their child's neck. The necklace symbolized health, prosperity and love. We felt it would be a way to honor the heritage of people who worked at the orphanage and thank them for taking such wonderful care of our daughter. By 3:30 p.m. we were in a taxi on our way back to the airport to catch our flight to Guangzhou and then on to Changsha.

The airports in China are not like airports in the United States. They are very confusing with rows and rows of counters. Each counter has one flight assigned to it. That wouldn't have been such a problem for us except that, of course, everything was in Chinese! I instantly had a new compassion for how visitors from other countries must feel when they came to the United States!

Bill and Gloria had joined us so the four of us began the process of trying to find the check-in counter for our flight. We finally found the right one, not by being able to read the sign above it, but by seeing four other American couples standing in the line. We assumed that they must be the other couples in our group, and we were right. After we introduced ourselves we started through the maze of checkpoints. We had to pass through three different security stations. The sensors were very sensitive, and we ended up being frisked at every station. We finally arrived at our gate and learned the *second* different thing about Chinese airports; there is *no* boarding protocol. No pre-boards, no row by row, just everyone pushing for the door at the same time. It was a normal process to the locals, but we were a little overwhelmed. You learn quickly that in China personal space doesn't mean much and assertiveness is the key to getting anywhere. We jumped in and started pushing our way through the crowd and boarded buses that took us out to our plane. Once settled into our seats on the plane we all commented about how different it was to hear the flight attendants giving instructions and announcements in a different language.

The flight itself was very short, just half an hour. We gathered our luggage and headed toward customs. We were surprised and thrilled to see Mr. Wu waiting for us. We were so thankful, because we knew we were now in safe hands. He welcomed us to China and led us out of one terminal down a road and into another terminal where we would board our plane to Changsha. We must have been quite a sight to the locals, because we looked like a group of ducklings following their Mama duck. What made it an even funnier sight was that each couple had between five and eight large pieces of luggage. People stopped to look at us in amazement. I realized later that we must have looked pretty ostentatious. The people of China on a whole do not have much in the way of personal belongings, so to see our group with all that luggage must have been a bit much for them.

As we took off I looked at a couple of the ladies in our group and commented that within an hour we would be in the same city as our daughters and within the next 24 hours, they would be in our arms. No one had to reply; their huge smiles said it all.

God, your Word says that You are faithful. I choose to believe that no matter what the circumstance may be, no matter what trial I may be experiencing I will stand in the knowledge that You are faithful to me and that Your Word will bring me truth, hope and a bright future. I am not alone.

The God Who Never Leaves Us

Deuteronomy 31:6

Be strong and courageous. Do not be afraid or terrified because of them, for the Lord your God goes with you; He will never leave you nor forsake you.

CHAPTER 17

Our plane touched down in Changsha, China, at 9:45 p.m. As we deplaned it didn't take long for us to realize that we were now in a very different part of China. The night air was bitterly cold, and there was no jet way to walk through or bus to take us to the terminal; everyone walked. As we headed toward the building we noticed that even though it was very dark outside none of the lights were on inside the terminal.

As we entered we saw one small ceiling light in the baggage claim area. We gathered our group under that light while we waited for Mr. Wu to tell us what we needed to do next. Since we were the only Americans on the flight there was a lot of chattering and pointing by the locals that let us know *we* were the topic of their conversations. As we heard the luggage start coming up the conveyor belt we were introduced to lesson number *three* about Chinese airports; don't stand next to the baggage carousel when the luggage comes out.

As soon as the first piece arrived the carousel was absolutely swarmed by the passengers. It looked like bees drawn to the beehive!

With all the luggage we had to gather we decided the best thing to do was wait until all the other passengers had retrieved their bags. That was a smart move, because it took us about 30 minutes to get all the luggage and load it onto carts. Mr. Wu directed us to the buses that were about a half-mile from the terminal. When the bus drivers saw all of us loaded down with luggage I think they were in shock; the looks on their faces were priceless. They stood there for a few minutes taking in the sight of all those suitcases, trying to figure out how in the world they were going to get them all onto the small buses. We women decided to let the men handle it, and we climbed on the bus to get out of the cold. By the time everything was loaded onto the bus everyone was exhausted and we couldn't wait to get to the hotel and get a good night's sleep.

We had an hour-long drive to the city down very bumpy roads. We listened to our guide as he officially welcomed us to his hometown. Alan (his American name) was twenty-three years old and was absolutely delightful. His name in Chinese meant "happy bell," and it was a perfect fit for him. We would become very attached to him over the next five days. Alan was proud of his city and of his home country, and as we listened to him describe Changsha we were impressed by his knowledge and the obvious pride he had for his homeland.

We finally arrived at the hotel and checked into what would be our home for the next five days, The Hutian Hotel. Alan told us that it was a four star hotel currently under renovation to become a five star. It was being beautifully decorated for the Chinese New Year in two weeks. Since it would be the year of the Ox they had a huge golden ox statue in the lobby. There were red and gold decorations everywhere; it was just beautiful. After everyone got checked in we made our way up to the seventeenth floor. Thankfully, all of us were on the same floor and the same wing in one large block of rooms. Each floor had an attendant who would bring you anything you needed including hot and cold boiled water because, like in other countries around the world, the water was not safe for us to drink.

We would spend the next two weeks trying to remember not to put our toothbrushes under the faucet and keeping our mouths closed in the shower. We also had to get used to rinsing out our mouths with hot water – yuck!

We bid each other a quick good night and got ready for a much needed night's sleep. The rooms were adequate with two twin beds, a large chest of drawers and a television. The hotel had also arranged to have cribs in all our rooms. The cribs were small metal beds with sides and a foam rubber mattress wrapped in a blanket. We quickly unpacked and hit the bed around 2:00 a.m. Sleep came quickly.

January 27 THE day. The phone awakened us at 6:30 a.m. We were to be ready to leave the hotel by 8:30 a.m. Todd and I rolled out of bed wondering if we had really slept or if we had just imagined it. After a quick shower and getting dressed we met everyone in the hotel's main restaurant to have breakfast together. It was a western style buffet and had everything you could want as well as lots of yummy Chinese dishes. We reintroduced ourselves and began the process of bonding as a group; it didn't take long. Everyone was so nice, and we all got along together very well. Alan and Mr. Wu met us at 8:30 a.m. to begin the final steps of the adoption process. After one last trip upstairs to get the needed gifts and money we left the hotel.

As we drove to our first destination Mr. Wu filled us in on the day's schedule. We were heading first to another hotel to be interviewed by the local adoption officials. The next stop would be the notary offices for another interview. After that interview we would go to lunch, swing by the hotel to gather the necessary things for the babies and head to the orphanage to be united with our daughters.

The Chinese officials met us at the hotel and escorted us into a room that was set up for the interviews. They decided it would be easier to talk to two couples at a time, so as two couples went back the rest of us waited in the lobby.

We decided to find a coffee shop and visit until we were called for our interviews. We had a wonderful time visiting but began to get restless as time passed. We were very nervous about this first interview, because we had heard they could be intense and the officials were intimidating and aloof.

After almost an hour Alan came out with a stack of paperwork for us to fill out. He began to interpret each line of the forms for us, so that we could complete them before our interview. I noticed earlier in our trip that the Chinese have certain symbols that stand for month, date and year, so when he reached the portion that pertained to our daughter's birth date I filled the dates in next to each symbol. Unfortunately, the others did not know the symbols. They assumed the symbols were instructions and skipped the line entirely. It was not until they had progressed about three more lines that they realized they had skipped a line and that their answers were now off by one line. A wave of panic ensued because the officials were known to be very particular about how documents are completed and allow for no errors on the originals that were to be turned in to the government. There were six very worried people sitting around that table fearful that they had put the adoption process in jeopardy.

Alan went back into the interview room to ask for help. The orphanage director's assistant came out and after a few more tense moments found new forms for them to complete. Crisis averted!

After we completed all the paperwork we waited about twenty minutes until the two couples came out grinning and carrying their daughters' official adoption decrees. Two more couples went next and we pumped the first two for all the details of what had happened during their interview. They explained that they had filled out their forms in the room with someone who did not speak English very well, and it had just taken a long time to translate the forms so they could be completed. They explained the entire procedure and remarked on how cordial and cooperative all the Chinese officials had been. That was great news to the rest of us!

After just twenty more minutes they called for us. We were ushered into the room by Mr. Wu and at one end of the room there were three desks. At two of those desks were local officials who would interview each couple. At the third table was the man who would take care of the fees we would pay that day. At the other end of the room was a couch where the orphanage director, his assistant and Mr. Wu sat.

The director was a very solemn man. His assistant on the other hand was delightful. She had short black hair, big red-rimmed glasses and a huge smile that lit up the room, and she always seemed to be laughing. The man who interviewed us asked the basic questions: name, age, hometown, occupation and financial status. He also asked if we had other children and asked their ages. When he finished he asked one final question, "Will you promise to never abandon or forsake your daughter, Liu Xi?" Our answer was an emphatic "YES."

He stamped our paperwork and gave us that precious piece of paper that was the official adoption decree. We thanked him for his time, paid the cashier and gave gifts to all the appropriate individuals. We went to the coffee shop to join the rest of the group and show off our decree. Mr. Wu came out and quickly ushered us to the buses, because the first set of interviews had taken so long we were over an hour behind schedule for our next meeting at the notary office. This presented two problems; the first was if we didn't meet with the notary today it would push all our other scheduled appointments to the next day. With the Chinese New Year starting the day after we were to leave there was no leeway for that type of delay. The second problem was that Mr. Wu had forgotten to tell us that we needed two more gifts for the notary officials. We quickly decided that the men would go with Mr. Wu to the notary office while the women would go back to the hotel with Alan to get the needed gifts.

We retrieved the needed gifts and left the hotel to meet up with the men at the notary office. On the bus we wondered how the men were doing with all the paperwork. It took almost an hour to get back and the men were *very* relieved to see us return. There were several key questions the men hadn't been able to answer. We just laughed as the men all started asking the same questions, "*What's her Chinese name?*" "*When was she born?*" and my personal favorite, "Did we decide on a name yet?"

I went into the room where Todd was trying his best to answer all the questions. It was difficult for him, because the official spoke no English and our translator wasn't that great at it either. At one point the official spoke to us in Chinese for quite a long time looking very serious. The translator turned to us and said, "She says that under Chinese law, you are not allowed to adopt a baby." Todd and I looked at each other in shock, and I think our hearts stopped at the same time. After several tense moments, the translator finally finished by saying, "but we have decided to allow you to adopt this child, Liu Xi." As soon as our hearts began beating again we were able to relax the death grip we had held on the arms of our chairs. I am sure we left permanent marks in those chairs!

The official looked at Netanya's picture for a few minutes and told Todd, "She looks like you." Although in the physical realm, her comment sounded very silly, to *us* it was yet another confirmation that God had created Netanya in every way just for our family. We were very proud parents. As the official stamped the documents we let out a cheer. Netanya Jade Stone was now legally our daughter. All that was left was to have her placed in our arms. The anticipation was building minute by minute as the parents shared a group hug and left the office. It was finally time to go get our daughters.

God, your Word says You will never leave me alone. I choose courage. I choose to stand even in the midst of an uncertain time, because I know that You will be with me through it all. I am not alone.

The God Who Completes Us

Philippians 1:6

He who has begun a good work in you will be faithful to complete it.

CHAPTER 18

After a quick lunch at a local restaurant we headed back to the hotel to prepare for **the** event. We went to our rooms to get diaper bags, blankets and a change of clothes for the baby. We also got the financial donations for the orphanage, the humanitarian relief we brought and video cameras with lots and lots of film. Even though we had all been talking nonstop since we got to Changsha, the silence now was deafening. It was evident that each couple had drawn deep within themselves, possibly reliving the steps of their own journeys to this point. It was almost unimaginable that we were finally here. Finally, we were at the place where for so long we had prayed to be. My stomach was in knots, my hands were shaking, and my mind was reeling. In the birthing process, I knew I was officially "in transition."

Alan met us outside the hotel, and we all boarded the bus. He explained that we would have the privilege of actually going to the orphanage to meet our daughters. This was uncommon during this period of time. Most adoptive parents were united with their children at their hotel, so we were thrilled to actually see where our daughters had spent the first few months of life. During the twenty-minute ride to the orphanage each couple sat close together holding hands. The emotional level was very high, and if anyone had said much tears probably would have flowed. Alan snapped all of us out of our thoughts when he said, "Here we are. Look to the left. There is the arch entrance to the orphanage." We all gazed out our windows looking at the white brick arch that led into a large grassy area inside the complex. Directly in front of us was a six-story, white brick building.

Our *daughters* were inside that building and for a moment we all sat motionless. The dads finally grabbed the video cameras and began filming the buildings and surrounding areas. Mr. Wu stood up and told us to follow him up to the orphanage conference room where the caretakers would be with our daughters. I felt as if I was in the delivery room, and my doctor had just told me to start pushing!

As we got off the bus I looked up at the building and saw someone holding up a small baby to the window. I turned around to the group and shouted, "Look! They are holding up our daughters!" There in the window one by one, six little girls were being held up for us to see. They were several stories up so it was difficult to see their faces clearly but when the third little girl was held up, I *knew* it was Netanya. I turned to Todd and yelled, "Todd! Todd! It's Netanya! Look!" He turned the camera around and began filming her from the window. We all stood there for a few minutes just watching all those beautiful little girls in the window, until finally Mr. Wu said, "Wouldn't you like to go up and actually *hold* your daughters?" We all took off for the door as quickly as we could!

The stairs were small and steep, and as we made our way up to the third floor my heart felt as if it was going to explode. When we reached the top of the stairs we were led into a large conference room with an oblong wooden table in the middle and small red velvet chairs all around the perimeter. Standing by the windows was the orphanage director, his assistant, the nurse, a notary official and the financial director. Sitting in the chairs were six caretakers and six of the most beautiful little girls you will ever see. Words failed us.

We all stood against one wall waiting for someone to tell us what to do. After what seemed like a lifetime, Mr. Wu spoke to the director in Chinese. He laughed and turned to us and said, "they think it would be fun for you to try to pick out your daughters." Since we only knew our daughters from a miniature picture that was taken over five months before we were all slightly taken aback. We certainly didn't want to make a mistake! But there was no doubt in my mind or Todd's. I immediately pointed to the fourth little girl in the chairs and said, "that's her. That's *our* daughter." Todd immediately agreed and Mr. Wu went over to the caretaker and asked her for the girl's name. The caretaker smiled and said, "This is Liu Xi."

Time was frozen for a moment as I looked at my daughter. People asked me later how I knew she was mine. "It was easy," I said, "it was her eyes." In her eyes I saw me, but more than that I saw *Jesus*. The presence of the Lord was all over her. She positively glowed. As I stretched out my arms to receive this *God provided priceless one* my heart melted. The caretaker placed her gently in my arms and smiled through her tears. The world stood still, and I drank in the smell of this tiny miracle that God had so graciously blessed us with. I had just given birth.

She was incredible, formed in the very image of God. Petite, dark-skinned, huge dark eyes, and dressed in a pretty pink outfit. Her eyes seemed to pierce through my whole being. There was no expression on her face just those eyes. As I held her close to my heart I stroked her hair. I whispered her name in her ear over and over and told her how much we loved her and how much God loved her. I told her that she had been created especially for us and that she was a true miracle. And then I just wept.

I took out the jade necklace we purchased and carefully placed it around her neck. The caretaker was very moved that we would honor this cultural tradition and beamed as she showed the other caretakers. Todd had been videoing the whole time, and it took me a few minutes to even realize he was there. I took the camera from him and placed his daughter gently in his arms.

As I started the camera I prayed that the video would turn out, because I couldn't see anything through my tears. Todd cradled her in his arms and whispered his love to her. The joy was overwhelming and the thankfulness we felt was indescribable. Our journey had finally ended. She was in our arms where she belonged and just where God had always intended for her to be.

As we began to look around the room at the other couples we were overwhelmed with what we saw. There was Kimberly with Bill and Gloria, resting in her mother's arms holding tight to her finger and smiling. Baby Anna was totally engulfed in her daddy's arms, so little and beautiful. Lilian was already fast asleep in the arms of her dad, her cheeks bright red and her thick black hair wet with perspiration. Katie, with eyelashes so long you could have braided them and eyes so big they took your breath away, was sitting contentedly in her mom's lap. Tess, chubby cheeked and frightened, was crying as her parents tried to comfort her. By the time we left, she too would be fast asleep in her mother's arms, legs dangling and hands clutching her mommy's shirt. They were six miracles straight from the hand of God.

We spent the next forty-five minutes taking pictures, admiring each other's babies and trying to communicate with the caretakers. It was a wonderful, wonderful time for everyone in that room. Finally, Alan asked that we all be seated so the doctor could tell us about different medications some of the children were taking. Katie, Anna, and Tess were taking some form of medication for an illness. We all listened intently as Alan translated for the parents and then shared with us about each baby's feeding and sleeping schedules. Netanya was eating seven to eight bottles a day and sleeping through the night. Todd put all the humanitarian aid we brought on the table and described the medications to the doctor. Alan translated for him and the doctor was very appreciative and overwhelmed by the amount of medication we provided. We were just glad to know that the babies who remained would have the much-needed supplies to keep them healthy and strong.

After about an hour, Mr. Wu told us it was time to go. The caretakers gave each of their children a final hug, and we were escorted out the door, down the stairs and back into the sunshine. It was one of the only times our daughters had ever been outside, and as we each came out of the staircase Mr. Wu took our pictures in front of the place where we were united together for the first time as families. We gazed around the orphanage one more time wondering how many other children were still upstairs dreaming of the day when a mommy and daddy would come for them. We drove slowly through the arches capturing on film the last glimpses of the only home our daughters had known. Todd whispered to Netanya, "Never again, sweetie, never again. You will never again be an orphan."

Silence filled our bus, as each couple soaked in the sight of the gift that was now snuggled tightly in their arms. Mr. Wu and Alan quietly watched us, taking in the overwhelming emotion of the moment. God's promise fulfilled. No words could express the gratitude I felt for my Heavenly Father. No more waiting, the sun had just broken through.

God, your Word says You will complete the good work You have started in my life. I choose to believe this, because You are a faithful, loving Father who loves me and desires the very best for me. I am not alone.

The God Who Ordains Our Days

Jeremiah 29:11-13

For I know the plans I have for you," declares the Lord, "plans to prosper you and not to harm you, plans to give you hope and a future. Then you will call on Me and come and pray to Me, and I will listen to you. You will seek Me and find Me when you seek Me with all your heart.

CHAPTER 19

We arrived back at the hotel and went to our rooms to bond as families. The first thing we wanted to do was get her out of all the layers she was dressed in so that we could get a good look at our daughter! The Chinese had a custom of dressing their children in multiple layers. They believed that the more clothing the child had on the less likely they were to get sick.

As I took off layer after layer Todd recorded the procedure, and we laughed as she kept getting smaller and smaller. The outer layer was a pretty pink outfit and underneath that was a very thick quilted two-piece outfit. A knitted red overall type outfit followed that layer. Next was a thin cotton one-piece outfit and finally another quilted two-piece suit. All that was left now was a diaper and three pairs of socks. When we got down to bare skin, we were amazed at how dark and beautiful her skin was. There were scars over a lot of her body from some type of infection but other than that she was very clean with no rashes or other skin disorders. I took her in the bathroom and held her close for several minutes. We ran a bath for her and she whimpered as I sponged her off with a warm cloth. After putting on lotion, powder and a diaper, we dressed her in pink ruffled pajamas.

As we sat with her we noticed that she had two unusual mannerisms that were so endearing. The first was a continual wave with her left hand. No matter what she was doing, her left hand was constantly waving, and it made her look like Miss America waving to her adoring crowd. The other mannerism was that she sucked her two middle fingers, so it looked as if she were signing, "I love you." We sat in awe as she lay on the bed quietly looking at us with those incredible dark brown eyes. When Todd picked her up to hold her she gave us the biggest thrill of our lives; she smiled. Two dimples framed her smile and her eyes seemed to come to life.

The next few hours were spent watching her and observing her developmental skills. She was very alert, could track objects well and looked for things if they disappeared from view. She had four teeth, two on the top and two on the bottom. Her motor skills were definitely lacking, but we were pleased at what we saw. She could roll from front to back and even managed to push herself up a little. She had no neck or back strength and she could not hold her head up for any length of time. There was no indication of a clubfoot. Her favorite position to be held was up on my left shoulder all cuddled up, so she could look out, suck those fingers with one hand and wave with the other. We were happy and relieved that she seemed to be well taken care of and had minimal developmental delays.

The highlight of that time together was when I was finally able to sing her song to her. I had waited fourteen long months to look in those eyes and sing to her the words of love and destiny that God was speaking over her. It was an emotional and spiritual experience for Todd and me. As I sang the words to her she seemed mesmerized and sat motionless in my arms quietly cooing. Todd prayed the most anointed prayer over her as he committed her to the Lord and sealed her place in our family. The air in the room was thick with the presence of the Lord. It was a moment I will never forget. For the second time that day, time stood still.

That evening we gave her a bottle, rocked her to sleep and put her in the crib for the night. She went right to sleep, and Todd and I emailed everyone back home with an update of the day's events. We sat for a while talking and watching her sleep, took a quick shower, crawled into bed and thanked God once again for the beautiful child that lay sleeping peacefully at the side of our bed.

January 28 That morning we dressed Netanya in a frilly pink outfit complete with matching headband. Thanks to all our friends back home we had headbands for every outfit that little girl wore. I had waited for nine years to have a baby girl to dress up, and I was determined to enjoy every moment of it! After she gulped down her bottle we went downstairs to join everyone for breakfast.

We were glad to hear that almost all the babies slept through the night. Katie was pretty sick, so her dad and mom decided to stay back in their room for the day. Alan told us he would take us to the local Friendship Store just down the block. The store was like a large department store in the United States. It was a five-story building that had everything from food to furniture all under one roof.

We all went back upstairs to get the baby gear we would need for our first official outing as a family. Gladney had suggested that we bring papoose packs to carry the girls in, and when we stepped outside that morning we found out very quickly why they had. We stuck out like a sore thumb and one of the men in the group smiled and said, "Welcome to the goldfish bowl!"

The store was only three or four minutes away but it took us over 45 minutes to get there. We were stopped multiple times by people in the street wanting to know two things. The first question we got asked was if our babies were boys or girls. The Chinese were very adamant that "outsiders" not adopt boys because they needed the boys to stay in country to grow up and eventually take care of their parents. Once the locals understood they were all girls they would begin to smile and say, "Lucky baby."

The second thing they wanted to know was if we were dressing the babies "appropriately." Most of the time, we failed the second requirement miserably. It was a cultural difference we just had to adjust to. Over the next two weeks we were scolded, poked, and glared at for not having the babies dressed in enough layers. The locals spent a lot of time tugging at our babies' clothes, trying to cover up any exposed skin or taking our blankets and rearranging them properly around the girls to cover them.

Once we finally reached the Friendship Store we were enthralled by what we saw. There was literally everything you could ever need there. We spent about an hour in the store but most of that time was spent standing still while crowds gathered around us. It was evident that the Chinese people loved their children. Most of the people seemed genuinely happy that we were adopting these little ones, and they knew that the girls would have a much better life with us.

It is such a difficult situation for the people of China whose love for children was obviously there but the ability and right to keep those children had been taken away. At one point we were walking down the street and Todd said, "I can't help but wonder how many of the women we pass by on these streets have had to give up their babies. I wonder if we have walked by Netanya's mother on these very streets." Wherever Netanya's mother was during the time we were there, we prayed that somehow she would know that her daughter would be loved and cherished and that knowledge would bring her true peace.

That afternoon as Netanya slept, Todd and one of the other dads decided to go explore the "real" Changsha. They spent over two hours walking through the city, taking pictures and trying to communicate with the locals. At one point they tried to go into a very impressive looking building but a soldier kept gesturing for them to stop. They thought he was trying to tell them to put away their cameras, so they did and proceeded to try to walk in again.

The soldier got very angry and forced them away. It wasn't until later that they found out the building was a Chinese military intelligence office. We gave the guys a hard time about almost getting arrested inside China. When we emailed our church friends back home about the adventure we got a return email that said, "We are so glad Todd didn't get arrested. It would have been really tough to explain that to the congregation!"

Wednesday, January 29 It had been a tough night. Netanya started getting fussy late in the evening and would not take her bottle at bedtime. She spent most of the night crying and in obvious pain. It was frustrating not knowing what was really wrong, so I just held her, sang to her and prayed over her. The next morning she seemed to perk up a little and even drank four ounces of formula. We decided to try to go with the rest of the group on a sightseeing trip of Changsha. We went to several interesting places rich in history and Alan did a wonderful job explaining the significance of each place. Todd took lots of pictures so that Netanya would have visual references of her birthplace. About halfway through the tour I could tell she was starting to feel poorly again. By the time we returned to the hotel she was exhausted and crying. She fell asleep on the bed, and I decided to make a phone call home to a doctor friend of ours.

As soon as I heard his voice I began to cry. I suddenly felt so isolated halfway around the world, in a strange land with a sick baby that I really didn't know anything about! We talked for several minutes about her symptoms and he gave me some suggestions on how to help her. He felt like the soy formula we were using might be causing some intestinal distress, so he advised us to find a milk-based formula. He prayed for Netanya over the phone, and I felt more confident and reassured as I hung up the phone. I was so thankful for praying friends and the reminder that even though they were half a world away we weren't in this alone.

When the rest of the group got back from lunch I told them what our friend had suggested. They all immediately pitched in to help. Several of them had the right kind of formula I needed and offered it to us. They reassured and encouraged us that everything would be fine and that they were all there to help with whatever we needed. The rest of the day was spent trying to help Netanya feel comfortable.

She finally fell asleep around nine that night and Todd and I sat down to write an email home asking for prayer for her. She slept until five the next morning, finally took a bottle of formula and then slept again until nine. We breathed a sigh of relief and thought our troubles were over. We didn't know they were just beginning.

God, your Word says that You have a prosperous and hopeful future for me and that You listen when I call out to You. When I am burdened, worried, frightened or confused I choose to call out to You. I choose to have an intentional prayer life and seek after You with all my heart. I am not alone.

The God Who Heals Our Heart

Psalm 55:22

*Cast your burden on the Lord, and He will sustain you;
He will never permit the righteous to be moved.*

CHAPTER 20

Thursday, January 30 The morning started out pretty well, Netanya seemed content and in no pain. The orphanage director and the doctor were coming over at noon to check on Katie and her. By the time they arrived Netanya was in distress again and seemed to be getting worse. The doctor examined her and concluded that her illness was being caused by not having enough layers of clothes on. I stood there looking at Alan who was translating for us and didn't even know what to say to him. It was definitely a moment of extreme cultural differences. He left without another word. We went back to our room and were finally able to rock her to sleep. She slept for several hours and woke up once again appearing to feel much better.

Later that afternoon the director came back to bring us something we had all been waiting for, the official adoption certificates. The girls were now officially *and* legally ours. Then the director shared with us information regarding each girl's abandonment. Netanya had been abandoned on August 2 in the middle of the night at the local police station. We were stunned to learn that her mother had kept her for almost two months. The heartache that mother must have gone through as she left her beautiful daughter on the stairs of the police station was a pain I could never fathom. For the privilege we now had of calling her our daughter it was also a debt I could never repay.

With the certificates safely tucked away everyone decided to go out to celebrate. I sent Todd with the group but Netanya and I stayed at the hotel to rest. The wear and tear on me emotionally and physically was starting to take its toll and my heart ached every time she cried. Fear began to creep in that I would not be able to provide the comfort my sweet daughter needed. But as we rested in the room that afternoon God calmed my fears in a sweet, sweet way.

Before we left for China I packed a few praise and worship tapes. That afternoon the Lord gently reminded me that the best way to fight off fear and frustration was to draw close to Him. I got one of the worship tapes out and as song after song filled my ears and my spirit, the fear began to lift. Within a few minutes I was literally dancing around the room singing at the top of my lungs (well at least inside my head I was) because Netanya had fallen fast asleep on the bed! The presence of the Lord was overwhelming. Rivers of refreshment swept over the darkness that had been present just a few minutes earlier. There was new life in that room and within me.

That afternoon we had a surprise call from friends back home. They called to tell us that our pastor had read our email to the Wednesday night group at church and that they were all interceding on our behalf. We were again reminded of how far and deep and wide the love of our Heavenly Father is for us.

January 31 It was finally time to leave Changsha. We were all ready to take the next step that would move us closer to home. Next up was Guangzhou, China to obtain the girls' VISAs. We had an appointment at the American Consulate in two days, and we couldn't wait to get there. We heard that the hotel would be a "little slice of Paradise" and we all agreed that after the last week we could sure use a little paradise right about now!

Alan wanted to take us on a walk that last morning to show us the local street markets. Netanya was feeling well enough to go out, and I was excited to be able to explore some of the city. It was a rather chilly day so we made sure to bundle up the babies to avoid being corrected by the locals. We were all growing a little weary of the attention, but unfortunately the locals had not grown weary of us! By the time we reached the end of the block there was a swarm of people around us. At times there were close to sixty people pushing in toward us asking questions, touching the babies and pulling the blankets up around them. For the first time we started to actually feel a little fearful. The women decided it would be wise to head back to the hotel and prepare for the afternoon trip.

After lunch we loaded up the buses and started toward the airport. Before we did there was one more stop we wanted to make, the police station where some of the girls had been abandoned. Alan arranged for us to be able to go there and take a few pictures. We pulled up the narrow street to the front of the station and sat quietly for a minute or two. I once again thought about the mother who had carried her child for nine months, had given birth and experienced the joy of seeing her daughter for the very first time and yet had to abandon her knowing she would never see her again. My heart broke for her.

Todd and I carried our daughter up those cold, hard stairs and held her close as we took a picture in front of the police station sign. We were allowed to go inside for a brief moment, and we thanked the officers for allowing us to come. They seemed genuinely touched as they looked at each of the babies cuddled contentedly in their mother's arms. As we boarded the bus I paused. I looked back at those steps and drew Netanya up as close as I could to my heart. I whispered into her ear that she would never be abandoned or forsaken again. I told her that God had created her in His image and that He was so proud of the person she would become. I thanked the Lord for allowing us to have her in our lives, and I promised Him that I would raise this beautiful little girl to His glory and for His purpose. And once again I wept for the mother who had to turn and walk away from this beautiful brown-eyed little miracle and never look back.

On our way to the airport Alan told us that he had a special surprise for us. He told us he was majoring in music at the local college and wanted to sing a song for us. As he sang the familiar tune "Auld Lang Syne," we all sat in awe of the beautiful voice he possessed. It was a very tender moment for all of us because Alan had become more than our guide in the last week, he had become family. We felt blessed to have his leadership and insight, and we were really going to miss him.

We arrived at the airport about an hour later. We knew by then that Chinese airlines "in country" didn't always arrive on time or leave on time either. They flew the planes when they wanted to, and if they chose not to fly, you stayed another night. We sent the men to check on our flight and the ladies went in search of a coffee shop. We found a restaurant upstairs and were seated in the back room. What ensued over the next twenty minutes could best be described as a Keystone Kops highlight reel.

We decided that we should order something to justify our sitting at such a large table in the restaurant, but unfortunately none of the staff spoke English. We tried to communicate with the waitresses in every way possible but to no avail. We finally gave up and began going around from table to table pointing at bowls of food that we recognized (or at least thought we did) and ordered one of each. By the time we were done we had no idea what, or how much, we had really ordered. The waitresses just stood there through the whole thing and giggled. The people at the other tables kept slapping our hands, because they thought we were trying to take their food. We must have looked ridiculous, but somehow we ended up with some pretty decent food! The men came up every few minutes with updates for us. Unfortunately, most of the updates were about more delays, but they finally came with the best news possible that our plane would leave in two hours. One of the couples had received a bottle of champagne on the flight over. They decided this was a perfect time to toast our new daughters. With thoughts of all that we had been through over the last year each of us raised our glass in thanksgiving for the beautiful treasures we had been given. And then, it was time to say goodbye to Changsha and Alan. As we gathered our belongings he leaned over to Todd and asked him if we knew the words to the song "Country Roads". We all did, so in the middle of a restaurant in the heart of China thirteen people sang with all the gusto we could muster and we sounded pretty good! As each of us went through the security checkpoint that would take us to our plane we hugged Alan goodbye and thanked him for everything he had done to make our stay in Changsha so comfortable. He just smiled and said, "Thank you for giving a new life to these little girls."

It was a quiet, easy flight and a little after 11:00 that night we touched down in Guangzhou and were met by our new guide. We could tell right away that he was not going to be like Alan. He was very businesslike and not much for small talk. Of course by then, neither were any of us. We went through the luggage retrieval process again and headed for our next hotel, The White Swan. The city of Guangzhou was much more westernized than Changsha and with the Chinese New Year coming there were thousands of beautiful white lights lining the road to the hotel. It really was quite breathtaking. By the time we checked into the hotel and got our luggage up to the rooms it was 1:00 in the morning. We quickly unpacked a few necessities, put Netanya to bed and collapsed into ours. Sleep once again came quickly.

February 1 That morning we met downstairs for breakfast. The White Swan was a big improvement over the hotel in Changsha. There were several western style restaurants and shops in the lower levels, a beautiful waterfall in the center and small ponds in the lobby area. It lifted our spirits as we began this last leg of our journey.

Our agenda for the day was to go to the local medical center where each baby would be given a physical exam to ensure they were healthy enough to travel. Then we would get their pictures taken for their VISAs. Our guide wasn't quite sure what we were supposed to do, so the paperwork took a little longer than it should have. We finally got everything filled out and began the exams, which were cursory at best. Height, weight, heart check, and then a quick look in the ears. Netanya weighed in at ten pounds two ounces and was twenty-six inches long and was pronounced "healthy to travel." The medical center and the shop for VISA pictures were within walking distance of the hotel, so we enjoyed the beautiful weather as we strolled down the busy streets. It was much warmer here and already in the seventies. It felt so refreshing! The VISA pictures took just a few minutes, and Netanya even managed a smile.

With our tasks completed, everyone decided to head off in different directions and get some shopping done. Todd and I headed back to the hotel to meet up with our missionary friend Carolyn again. She and her roommate were going to take us to see a pastor who had been imprisoned for over twenty-one years for trying to preach the Gospel. We were thrilled and honored to be able to meet him. The four of us took a taxi into the middle of Guangzhou, and then walked deep into the heart of the surrounding apartments and office buildings. The streets were very narrow with a lot of twists and turns, and we eventually walked up a small, dark alleyway to reach his apartment. We climbed a narrow flight of stairs and knocked gently on the door. A very pleasant looking lady answered the door and after visiting with our friend for a few minutes she invited us in. She informed us that the pastor was still taking his afternoon nap but that he would be up soon. She showed us to a table and asked us to wait there. The room was long and narrow and there were about twenty rows of short pews on each side. At the back of the room was a table filled with Chinese Bibles. There were several people at the table working on something and they would stop to look at us every once in a while. I think they were very intrigued by Americans holding a Chinese baby.

As we looked around we realized that the apartment had two floors with the floor below mirroring the floor we were on. There was also a closed circuit camera to video the sermons. We sat talking for a few minutes until a small, fragile man came up the stairs with a huge smile on his face. He welcomed us warmly and shook each of our hands. This was Samuel Lamb.

I had never heard the name before, but as I listened to his testimony I was overwhelmed with respect and admiration for him. He had been imprisoned for all those years just for preaching the Gospel. One of the saddest parts of his story was that just a few months before his release his wife died. He had tears in his eyes as he shared how close they had come to seeing each other again after all those years. But then he smiled and spoke of the joy that would come when they would be reunited in heaven. It was a privilege to have him share such a personal and private memory with us.

Pastor Lamb had overcome tremendous persecution and continued to preach the Gospel. He felt that persecution brought growth and he boldly said that he didn't care if he was arrested again. He told us that every time his church was raided or he was personally persecuted, his church grew and the Lord was glorified. He was currently holding four services a week and had over 1,600 people attending those services. He shared several pamphlets with us that shared his personal testimony and included many of his teachings. He also gave us audiocassettes of songs the Lord had given to him while he had been in prison.

He told us that in all the years he was imprisoned not *one time* did he ever feel alone. He said that God was his constant companion and that even during the most difficult of days he felt God's hand on him all the time. He knew he wasn't alone. He knew God's eye never wandered from him in that prison cell. And he never lost hope that God would free him from that cell. We were humbled and honored to be able to meet such an incredible man of God. The light of the Lord simply radiated from him. Before we left he took a picture with Netanya and then Todd had the privilege of praying for him. We left with a sense of awe and wonder that such a simple, gentle man could be such a spiritual giant in the hands of a mighty God.

The rest of the day was spent letting Netanya nap while we visited with the rest of the group. The hotel had put us together again, so we sat out in the hallways while the babies slept sharing more about ourselves and preparing for the last few days we had together in China.

By now we felt like a family. It saddened us to know that soon we would go our separate ways.

February 2 I spent the afternoon in the hotel room catching up on Netanya's journal as she slept. Todd and some of the other men took a taxi to go explore Guangzhou. As I watched our beautiful daughter sleep contentedly in her crib I thought back over the last few days and all the incredible changes that had taken place in her life. It was amazing to see how well each of the girls was adjusting. That day I wrote:

Journal entry:

"You are an absolute delight, Netanya. Your smile and laugh simply light up our day! You are so content to rest in our arms and simply watch the world. You take my breath away, and I can't believe the blessing I have received in you. My heart is so full of joy and gratitude. What the enemy meant for death, God has brought life. He has held you lovingly under His mighty wing until we could reach you, and He will continue to watch over you all the days of your life."

The enemy didn't like that much.

God, your Word says that I can cast all my cares on You. I choose to be willing to lay down all my hurts, disappointments, fears and frustrations at your feet and leave them there. I will let You carry the weight of those burdens, because You are more than able, and I will allow Your power to flow through me so that I will be immovable in my faith. I am not alone.

The God Who Comforts Us

2 Corinthians 1:3-4

Praise be to the God and Father of our Lord Jesus Christ, the Father of compassion and the God of all comfort, who comforts us in all our troubles, so that we can comfort those in any trouble with the comfort we ourselves receive from God.

CHAPTER 21

February 3 We spent the evening laughing and enjoying our time together as a group. We had been through so much together over the last two weeks and had grown very fond of each other. We weren't ready to say goodbye just yet. The babies had gone to bed, so the moms gathered out in the hallway to fill out the massive amount of paperwork needed for our interviews at the consulate the next day. After several hours we finally finished all the forms and went to bed with full hearts. At 2:00 in the morning Netanya woke up screaming, and I could tell she was in a great deal of pain. I tried to comfort her, feed her and rock her but nothing worked.

She spent the next six hours crying a cry that neither Todd nor I had heard before. We knew something was definitely wrong. I walked up and down the hallways of the hotel singing, praying and doing anything I could think of to comfort her. Morning brought no relief. She was getting worse, not only crying in pain but her stomach seemed to be in distress as well. She was doubling over and squirming constantly trying to get comfortable. We were all supposed to go out that morning on one last sightseeing trip, but I knew there was no way Netanya could handle it. We decided to send Todd with the group, and I would take Netanya to the hotel medical clinic. There was nothing more Todd could do, and I wanted to make sure we had all the pictures we could of her homeland. So Todd set off with camera in hand and Netanya and I headed down to the clinic. Speaking in broken English the nurse warmly greeted me. I gave her all the important information concerning Netanya, and she went in to translate for the doctor. After an examination the doctor gave her diagnosis to the nurse: two ruptured eardrums, ear infections and an intestinal infection, along with a case of bronchitis. The doctor wanted to give her two shots, but we had been warned not to allow them to do that due to the uncertainty of the sanitary conditions in this part of the world. Katie's mom had stayed at the hotel with me and came down to check on us. She saw how tired I was, assessed the situation quickly and politely explained to the doctor that we did not want the shots. The doctor wasn't thrilled with our decision, but bowed to our request and instructed the nurse to prepare four different kinds of medications to be given every three hours. She also tried to clean Netanya's ears, which was a total disaster. By the time the procedure was done Netanya was hysterical and I wasn't far behind.

When I finally left the clinic I went back to the room and broke down in tears and was still in tears when Todd returned. When I told him everything that had transpired at the clinic he wrapped me in his arms, reassured me and reminded me that we would be home soon. He prayed over us, and I immediately felt the warmth of heavenly arms wrapping themselves tightly around our family. Netanya fell asleep in my arms, exhausted from the strain of the last several hours.

After a short rest we pulled ourselves together for the consulate interview. We met in the lobby to walk next door and our guide showed the guard at the gate our passports. We were escorted into the compound past a large group of Chinese citizens. Once inside, our guide put us in a room as he tried to locate where we were supposed to go for our interviews. He came back several times obviously frustrated at his inability to locate the proper room, so we decided to try to find it on our own. We followed signs that led us to a reception area on the second floor and a woman there asked us who we were. We showed her our documents and she quickly escorted us into a large, comfortable waiting room.

The room was obviously set up for parents seeking VISA's for their babies, because there were cribs, toys and swings lining the walls. We sat down on the couches and waited for someone to tell us what to do next. Within minutes a gentleman walked in with folders in his hands, called out our names and the interview process began.

This specific interview was something else we had been warned about in advance. We were told that the consulate employees were not very pleasant and could make the interview difficult for all concerned. With that in mind, we were all on our best behavior.

The information we received couldn't have been more wrong. The people who helped us were very polite, considerate and cordial. The interview process consisted of two steps. The first was to give all our paperwork and documentation to a consulate officer. She checked it to make sure everything was there and then asked us to be seated for a few minutes. The second step was the actual interview and ours went something like this:

"Mr. and Mrs. Stone. Hi, my name is Jenny. Is this the little girl you are adopting? Great! How did you come up with the name Netanya? I always like to hear how people decide on unusual names like hers."

We told her how we had gotten the name and she replied,

"Well, it is certainly a beautiful name. She is a lucky girl. Mr. Stone, she looks like you. Well, I guess that's all I need. Come back tomorrow after three, and you can pick up her VISA then. Good luck."

It took a total of maybe two minutes. Todd and I got up looking at each other totally baffled. That was the feared interview? We were so relieved!

Within twenty minutes we were all on our way out the gates and back to the hotel. We were done. It was time to celebrate! Netanya was still feeling pretty poorly, so we spent the rest of the day letting her rest and giving her all the medicine she needed. Thankfully she slept most of the day. I couldn't wait to get on the next plane and get her home. One more day and we were on our way!

February 4 Today we would finish up last minute shopping, pack bags, and get the girls' VISAs. Netanya still wasn't feeling the best and all the medicine we had to give her was an ordeal in itself. Three of the medicines were liquid, but one of them was a pill that had to be crushed and dissolved. We had to fill the syringe four times to get all the medicine down, and she was in no mood to cooperate with the process.

The men went to get the VISAs while the women finished last minute packing. When they returned we met downstairs in the lobby to get pictures of all the girls together. It was adorable to see all those beautiful God-given miracles lined up on the couch with proud Papas clicking away with the cameras. And then it was time to go home.

Eight of us were flying to Shanghai that evening to catch flights home in the morning. The others were flying to Hong Kong in the morning and then home from there. We said tearful goodbyes to precious Tess, Anna and their parents. We had grown so close it was difficult to imagine that we might not ever see each other again, but we knew that our daughters would always hold special places in each other's hearts.

Our guide took the rest of us to the airport and almost before we knew it, we were on our way to Shanghai. One more stop and we would finally be headed to the good ole' US of A. Nothing had ever sounded so good! When we arrived in Shanghai one more guide met us and took us to our hotel. We didn't arrive until after midnight and by the time they got our luggage and a crib up to our room it was after 1:30 in the morning. We had to be back up at five thirty so we quickly crawled into bed to sleep for a few hours.

Morning came very quickly. We struggled out of bed, grabbed a quick shower and headed downstairs for a light breakfast before we went to the airport. As we boarded our flight bound for Tokyo I quietly prayed one more time for the mother who had given the ultimate gift to her daughter; the gift of life. And then it was finally time to say goodbye to China.

The flight to Tokyo was uneventful and was followed by "the wait." We had a five-hour layover before our flight to San Francisco. Bill and Gloria were flying all the way back to Grapevine with us, so we all sat around and waited. There wasn't a whole lot to do in the Tokyo airport but walk around and sit and we did lots of both. I had come as prepared as possible for Netanya. Since she was still struggling with being sick I brought lots of Pedialyte® and plenty of changes of clothes. Finally it was our time to board and we couldn't get on that plane fast enough. We settled in for the nine and a half hour flight hoping Netanya would sleep through a large portion of it. We figured she was probably pretty exhausted, we knew we were!

A lovely flight attendant came by and noticed Netanya right away and instantly fell in love with her. She spent the rest of the flight giving us all kinds of goodies and pampered us every time she could. But we also got our first taste of the cultural chasm that existed among some Chinese people. The attendant who was so enamored by Netanya was showing her off to everyone and walked over to a fellow flight attendant who happened to be Chinese. She showed Netanya to her and said, "Netanya, this is someone from your homeland. Look at what a beautiful girl you will grow up to be!" Without hesitation, the Chinese flight attendant snapped back, "I am American sweetie- don't lump me in with HER." Then she brushed by us and walked to the back of the plane. She spent the rest of the nine-hour flight ignoring us. We learned that her mother was a Hong Kong native and her father American. For some sad reason she was ashamed of her mother's heritage. I learned a valuable lesson that day. I didn't ever want Netanya to be ashamed of her heritage, and we were going to ensure that she grew up being proud of her home country and her birth mother and father who loved her enough to give her the chance of a better life.

We took off from Shanghai at 6:30 p.m. and spent the next three hours wishing we were anywhere but in a plane over the Pacific Ocean. Netanya's ears couldn't take the pressurized cabin, and she was in a great deal of pain. Unfortunately, for everyone around us she was not shy in letting us know how she felt. Nothing would comfort her. We tried everything, but there was no consoling her. I am sure the other passengers were dreading the thought of another six hours of a screaming baby on board but all we could do was walk the aisles of the plane. Every time we walked by Bill and Gloria we would look down at Kimberly who was fast asleep. It broke my heart knowing there was nothing I could do to comfort my daughter.

Netanya's pain finally took its toll on me. Todd found both of us in the back of the plane crying. I stood there with tears streaming down my face half from fatigue and half from a burdened heart for my daughter. True to form he lovingly told me to go sit down and rest. I was too tired to argue. I numbly ate my meal and tried to catch a bit of a nap. I woke up to Todd beside me with Netanya fast asleep on his shoulder. He had worked his magic on her, and I thanked God for my amazing husband. Todd and I dozed on and off for the next few hours.

The rest of the flight was long but quiet. She was fussy on and off but seemed to be in less pain, which eased our hearts a great deal. We had called ahead to friends who lived in San Francisco, and asked them to meet us at the airport with more Pedialyte®. As the plane touched down in San Francisco we let out a cheer to be back on American soil. We gathered our luggage and headed off to make our way through immigration and customs.

As we got in line Netanya decided she was done with all the travel. I must have felt the same way, because I grabbed the first customs agent I saw and talked him into heating up a bottle for her in their break room microwave. Risky move grabbing a federal agent but this Mama didn't care! We got through immigration and customs with no problems. I think they felt sorry for us! Todd looked at me and said, "That's it. We are done. No one can stop us now."

She is ours, ours, ours!" The smiles on our faces could have lit up the entire state of Texas.

Our friends were outside the customs area with their video camera running as we came through the double doors. They had a sweet little doll that played "Jesus Loves Me" and the all-important Pedialyte®. We had about a forty-minute wait until our next plane, so we decided to grab a bite to eat and visit. They could see how exhausted I was, so they offered to take Netanya for a while and I gladly accepted. I was weak from my own sickness that had started the day before and Netanya's pain had exhausted me emotionally.

They must have done some heavy duty praying over Netanya, because when they came back she was totally quiet and relaxed. She had finished off her bottle and was lying quietly on my friend's shoulder. We said our goodbyes and by the time we sat down in our seats Netanya was fast asleep. I laid her in the seat next to mine, and she didn't move a muscle. The flight attendant came by and told me I would have to hold her during takeoff. I looked at Todd with this horrified look on my face and he said, "Don't touch her. I'll handle it." He came back a few minutes later, and no one asked us to move her again.

The flight was three hours long and for two and a half of those hours Netanya slept without stirring. Todd and I were able to take short naps and relax a little. We knew that a few of our friends were going to meet us at the airport, so we were glad for the time to regroup and freshen up. But the enemy had one more trick up his sleeve.

God, Your Word says that You will comfort me in my time of need. I choose to look to you when I am overwhelmed and weak. I know that only You can place my feet back on solid ground and renew my strength. I am not alone.

The God Who Is True to His Word

Proverbs 30:5

Every word of God proves true; He is a shield to those who take refuge in Him.

CHAPTER 22

As we began our descent into DFW our hearts were beating with anticipation. Within a few minutes we would be reunited with Joshua and Jacob, our parents and our friends. We couldn't WAIT to be back home!

With perfect timing, Netanya finally woke up. This would allow me the chance to give her one more bottle and change her before we landed. She finished the bottle, and I was in the midst of changing her as the plane prepared to land. Suddenly, the engines of the plane roared to full throttle. The plane that just a few seconds earlier had begun to settle quietly down to the ground was now straining to stay in control as it went straight back up into the sky. The pressure change in the cabin was sudden and dramatic. All of us were literally sucked back into our seats. Netanya's ears must have felt as if they had exploded, because she let out a piercing scream that came from the depths of her being. The plane climbed into the night for several minutes and then slowly leveled off before beginning a second descent. Netanya screamed the whole time. Forget the change of clothes or anything else, I just held her close to me and prayed. After what seemed like a lifetime the plane finally touched down and everyone on board started cheering and clapping. I don't know if the cheering was to congratulate the crew or to give thanks that they would soon be off the plane with the crying baby. Within a few minutes we had taxied up to the jet way. We would find out later that our pilot realized at the last moment that there was a plane directly in front of us on the runway. If he had landed we would have collided with the other aircraft at full speed. All he could do was put everything into the engines and climb as quickly as possible. While the enemy planned for death God provided life once again. His promise would not be denied.

As we prepared to disembark the flight attendant came over to us and said, "I hope you guys are ready. They just told me on the phone that your whole church is out there." Todd and I looked at each other wondering what in the world she was talking about. As soon as we walked into the gate area we found out! There were over 150 people crammed into the lobby with cameras, balloons and signs. They all began clapping and cheering as soon as they saw us. It was truly overwhelming. We were not prepared for the outpouring of love we received that night. And bless her heart, Netanya cried through it all.

The first people we saw were Joshua and Jacob. They were standing in the doorway with huge smiles on their faces and tears in their eyes. My heart just burst with pride and joy as I pulled them close to me. I held my three miracles in my arms. People started to come forward with hugs, kisses and words of love. After twenty-seven hours of traveling we were home. All you had to do was look around and see the joy and excitement in the faces of our friends to know that God was in this place. It was incredible, and for the next forty-five minutes we were given a king's welcome. What a time of rejoicing it was! So many had encouraged, supported and prayed for us and here was the fruit of their prayers.

My mom finally stepped in and announced very politely but firmly, "Dana is tired. It is time to go home." Who's going to argue with a mother? So we made our way to the baggage carousel, retrieved our luggage and were on our way. Netanya decided she might as well cry all the way home too, so she did. We pulled up in our driveway only to find more balloons, banners and ribbons. Our home group had been very busy. It was so pretty and it made us feel so special and loved.

I felt as if I were walking in slow motion when I carried Netanya into her forever home. The last two weeks suddenly caught up with me, and I literally sagged under the weight of the emotions within me. All I wanted to do was get Netanya into her crib and fall into bed, but we had one more visitor coming. Our doctor friend and his wife were coming by the house to examine Netanya. Todd, his folks, my mom, the boys and I collapsed onto the couches to wait for them. Netanya rested quietly on my shoulder as we shared a little of the journey with our family. Our pastor, our doctor friend and his wife showed up about twenty minutes later.

He examined Netanya and confirmed the diagnosis that the Chinese doctor had given us. He gave us several antibiotics as well as eardrops to help speed the healing process. Before they left, we all gathered around as our pastor laid hands on Netanya and prayed over her. Par for the course she cried through it all. And then it was finally time. For sixteen months I had waited to rock my daughter, sing her to sleep and lay her in her crib. There was no stopping the tears as I sang her song to her in her very own room. She slowly drifted off to sleep, her little body curled up in a tight ball on my chest. As her breathing slowed to a peaceful rhythm I rocked her not wanting the moment to end. I laid her in her crib and silently watched her sleep for a few minutes. She was finally where God had always intended for her to be. Home.

The next few days we spent with just our immediate family. From the first moment they saw Netanya the boys had bonded with their new sister. They knew just how to comfort her, what to do to make her laugh and how she liked to be held. It took about a week for her to get on Texas time but after many nights of playtime at 2:00 in the morning she adjusted. God graced us with supernatural strength during that time, because somehow we never felt tired. We would laugh and play all through the night just delighted to have our daughter in our arms.

February 9 Our first Sunday back at church and what a day of rejoicing it was! When we walked into the church we were met with congratulations and hugs from everyone. There was so much to be thankful for and as the church service started we stood to give thanks to God for His ever-present hand on our lives. Once again the tears flowed with thanks and grateful hearts for the privilege of raising this beautiful daughter we held in our arms. Before he began his sermon our pastor stood and said, "We have a miracle right here among us today, and she has come all the way from China." He asked us to come up to the front, and as we did the congregation stood cheering and clapping to welcome our daughter to her new home.

God had promised me a rainbow, a miracle. He promised me the desires of my heart. As we stood before our church family that morning we rejoiced in the fulfillment of His promise. He had given us the desire of our hearts right on time. And there she was in my arms waving and smiling in her beautiful red velvet dress.

God, your Word says that You are true to Your Word. I choose to take refuge in Your arms and allow You to be my shield. I believe the Word of God is true yesterday, today and forever. I am not alone.

THE GOD WHO IS FATHER TO THE FATHERLESS

Matthew 19:14

Let the little children come to Me and do not hinder them; for the kingdom of God belongs to such as these.

CHAPTER 23

Our hearts were so full. Our beautiful daughter had been lovingly placed in her forever family. We were so very thankful that God would give us this amazing little girl to love. Over the next several months she quickly became acclimated and began to thrive. Winter became spring and spring summer. Before we knew it fall was approaching and that meant Operation Christmas Child! With all that we had just experienced and seen in China we had a renewed passion for sharing the Father's love with others.

We had seen first hand the need for ministries like OCC that brought hope and the love of Christ to so many children around the world. We had participated in OCC at our church in 1995 and collected a little over three hundred boxes that year. Now here we were two years later and we were an official collection center and collected over seven thousand boxes. Our volunteer base had grown as well. We had over fifty people from our church and surrounding communities who gave their time and efforts receiving, sorting, boxing and loading all the shoeboxes into semi tractor trailers. Todd and I were blown away by the support and the passion people had for this simple yet powerful ministry opportunity. As we wrapped up another successful year we got a surprise phone call from Ross Robinson. Ross was an Associate Pastor at a large church in Dallas that had been the only collection center for OCC for many years. He and I had become friends over the last two years as I became more involved in the ministry, and he had helped me through the process of becoming a regional collection center. He called me that day with news that shocked and thrilled Todd and I. Ross had arranged for us to be able to travel to Bucharest, Romania to be part of a team that hand delivered some of the thousands of shoeboxes to children in need. Here we were not even a year after coming home from China and now we would travel to Romania to be able to personally share love and hope to more children. So in January 1998, we left DFW bound for Bucharest with our three children safely nestled in the home of good friends.

We arrived in Bucharest and were taken to a beautiful hotel that we would call home for the next five days. That evening we had a team meeting where we met everyone and were given details about the places we would visit during our time there. We quickly realized there would be little down time during this trip and that we would have the privilege of visiting four different orphanages during our time there. We all got a good night's sleep so that we would be ready to go bright and early the next morning.

Our first visit was to a hospital that had been turned into an orphanage. Many of the children there were brought to the hospital to be tested for tuberculosis because one of their parents had contracted the disease. Unfortunately, many of the parents had either passed away or could no longer afford the cost of additional family members, so the children were abandoned and left to live at the hospital. Their home now consisted of a twin bed, a nightstand, a few items of clothing and either slippers or one pair of shoes. Handmade paper decorations and artwork hung above their beds and there were just a few books and toys to share among a hundred or more children. The staff provided for the children as best they could, but it was not an ideal situation.

As we handed out the shoeboxes to each child I watched as their eyes opened wide at the pretty wrapping paper that adorned the decorated boxes. They were overjoyed and sat down quietly just looking at the boxes. The amazing thing about watching them was that they didn't even realize that inside of each of those boxes were gifts just for them. They were thrilled just to receive a beautiful box! We had to open the lids of the boxes to show the children all the treasures inside waiting for them. The squeals and laughter that quickly filled the room were indescribable. Over the next hour we spent time with each child playing, laughing, hugging and loving on them. The once sanitary, stoic room had been transformed with the undeniable presence of the Lord. The sweetest moment came when we were able to share pictures and notes lovingly placed inside each box by the person who had packed the box. The children couldn't believe that someone they had never met would care enough to send them such a lavish gift. It was in that moment we were able to share the love of Christ with them. We were able to tell them about a God who loved them, who watched over them, who saw them. We told them about a love so deep that even death couldn't separate us from it. In that moment they saw a glimpse of eternity, many for the first time.

That scene was repeated time and time again over the next four days. In a Romanian orphanage funded by American missionaries, in an all girl's orphanage that housed the unwanted, gypsy children ranging in age from two to fifteen, and to an all boy's orphanage where the ages ranged from birth to fifteen. We learned that once they turned sixteen the children were dismissed from the orphanages and sent to live on the streets. Many of the children ended up living in the sewer systems below the streets or in doorways searching through garbage for food to survive. It was a dismal life from an earthly perspective, so to be able to give them a heavenly perspective was a powerful experience for all of us. I will never forget the sound of over a hundred and fifty young girls squealing with delight as they opened their boxes to discover the treasures within. It was a sound that will ring in my spirit for the rest of my life. Every place held a God moment; from a toy that spoke exactly to the need of a child, a prayer that ministered to a staff member or a song that reached across the cultures and turned us into a family. These are moments that I will cherish forever.

The final place we visited was the city hospital. We were divided into different teams and escorted to several different wings of the very large building. As we entered the wing on the fifth floor everything got very quiet. We knew immediately that this wing housed children with serious health issues. The doctors didn't say anything to us and quietly went about their work. Todd and I were led into a room at the end of the hallway that was dimly lit. A father and mother sat together in a chair close to the edge of the hospital bed and were obviously in great distress. As we came all the way inside the room we quickly realized that the young boy in the bed was in very bad shape. He lay naked in the bed, with no covering over him and was badly burned. One lone IV hung by his bedside and dripped medication to try to ease his pain.

Through our interpreter we learned that this was Alexander. He was 7 years old and had been left at home alone because both parents worked all day seven days a week to provide for Alexander and his younger brother. Three days earlier Alexander had tried to provide a hot meal for his younger brother and in the process the large frying pan with hot grease fell over on him. He had third degree burns over 50% of his body and was not expected to live. The parents were devastated and were overcome with guilt. We spoke quietly to them for a few minutes and found out both of them were Christians. When they found out we were Christians as well they begged us to pray for their son to be healed. I quickly gathered several team members, and we began to pray for Alexander. We prayed for healing, we prayed for protection from infection, we prayed for the pain to ease and we prayed for his parents. We prayed for their broken hearts, for the guilt they were experiencing, for rest and for wisdom. The Spirit of the Lord was so heavy in that room, and although we may never know the outcome of those prayers we know that God entered into that moment and the family felt the overwhelming love of Christ. They felt His arms of compassion wrap tightly around them, and they knew their son whatever the outcome, was not alone and neither were they.

We left Romania with our hearts full. It was yet another reminder that God cares about all of His children and desires to reach into any situation or life circumstance to show us just how much He loves us, that we are His and He is ours.

God, Your Word says that children are very important in Your eyes. I choose to believe that I am Your child and that You watch over me all the time. I know that no matter what happens in my life, You are there with me. I will call out to you without hesitation no matter the circumstance because I know You love me. I am not alone.

The God Who Loves Us Unconditionally

Ephesians 3:17-19

I pray that you, being rooted and established in love, may have power, together with all the Lord's holy people, to grasp how wide and long and high and deep is the love of Christ, and to know this love that surpasses knowledge—that you may be filled to the measure of all the fullness of God."

CHAPTER 24

Life as a family of five was absolutely amazing over the next two years. We loved watching Netanya soak up everything around her. It was so fun to watch her accomplish all the basics, like taking her first steps, enjoying holiday traditions and learning how to ride her first bike. The boys adored their sister and were constantly by her side cheering her on all the way. She was made for our family. She loved being outside, going to baseball games and singing in church with us. She was a Stone through and through and all of us marveled at how God had blessed us with this good and perfect gift.

When Netanya was two Todd and I decided it was time to find a bigger home for our family. We were in an eighteen hundred square foot house with only three bedrooms and one living area. With three active children and two very large German Shepherds it was time to move! Todd had started his own construction company and recently purchased some land to build a new office. Several times he noticed a beautiful home behind the property and commented to me that it would be so neat to live there and be able to walk through the back yard to his office each day. One day we decided to go knock on the door and visit with the owners to see if they might be interested in selling their home. They quickly welcomed us inside and within five minutes we felt an immediate kinship with them. They were a lovely Christian couple who had lived in their home for over twenty years but had no intention of moving. They were so gracious and took the time to show us the house and the beautiful front and backyards. The husband was an avid gardener and there were rows and rows of gorgeous rose bushes in the backyard that were immaculately kept. The house sat on one and a half acres and had a creek running through one side of the property. The long driveway was lined with forty-foot tall pine trees. Large trees and bushes surrounded the outskirts of the entire property. It was truly an oasis in the middle of our busy town.

After visiting for over an hour, we thanked them for spending time with us and gave them our phone number in case they ever decided to sell their home. They laughed and said so many others had asked them over the years that they could probably paper their walls with the business cards left behind. That evening Todd and I prayed that the Lord would open a door if that house were meant for us.

Life moved on and then one day two months later our phone rang. It was the owners of the home. They told Todd that as soon as we had left that day the Lord told them it was time to sell the house and that we were to be the new owners. It had taken them both so much by surprise that it took several weeks for them to make the decision to actually move. When they finally made the decision a new opportunity immediately presented itself to them in Oklahoma. They asked Todd if he was ready to buy the house. It didn't take us two months to think about it, and we said yes the next day!

There we were one month later packing up our home and moving into a two-story four thousand square foot house with over an acre of land for the kids and dogs. We were ecstatic. Todd's parents came up on June 19 to help with the move. Netanya's birthday was in two days, and she was so excited to celebrate her third birthday in our new home. The kids were most excited about the fact that each of them would have their very own room. They had shared rooms in various combinations over the last two years and couldn't wait to have a room to call their own! With the help of family and friends we managed to move our entire household to our new home in one day. That afternoon the ladies stayed at the new house to start unpacking, while the guys kept moving boxes. I was going up the stairs when suddenly I had a wave of nausea hit me so fast that I actually buckled. I sat there for a few minutes waiting for the feeling to pass. When I got up one thought ran through my mind, *I know this feeling. What is it?* Another wave hit me a few minutes later and I sat down on the floor in my bedroom trying to figure out what the feeling was and why it was so familiar. And then suddenly I knew.

I sat on the floor a few more minutes trying to convince myself that I was wrong and that I was just tired, but I knew. My mind was not yet ready to grasp the possibility, so I slowly made my way downstairs, got my car keys and told my mother-in-law that I was going to run to the store. As I made my way into the local convenience store every thought imaginable came to me in those few moments. *We are done, aren't we Lord? You gave me the desire of my heart. We have three amazing kids and an amazing new home. Everyone has their own room! There's no way. Right, Lord?"* So, with those questions reeling in my head I walked down the aisle, took a deep breath and picked up a pregnancy test.

When I got home I went back upstairs, took the test and sat back down on the floor to wait for the test results. My mind wandered back to that day in the doctor's office when our doctor asked Todd and I about having my tubes tied. I vividly remembered the words the Lord spoke to me that day, *"What about the miracles yet to come?*

Do you trust me?" I took a deep breath and with childlike faith said the only thing I could say, "Yes Lord. I trust you." I leaned over to look at the pregnancy test, and there it was, two bright blue lines. I was pregnant.

Time stopped for a few minutes. I really don't know what I did, but I do remember going downstairs finding my mother-in-law and pulling her into a room to tell her the news. How in the world was I going to tell my husband that all our plans for our new house had just been thrown out the window! We decided to go to a minor emergency clinic just to be sure before we dropped the bombshell on Todd. Off we went again and the result was indeed the same.

By the time we got home Todd and his Dad were at the house trying to figure out where we were. I smiled, sat my husband down at the kitchen table and told him exactly where I had been. He sat there for a few moments silently looking out the window into the backyard. After what felt like a lifetime he finally turned back to me with a smile on his face and said, "Babe we can always trust His plan for our lives. We're going to have another baby to love!" And so our new adventure began.

We settled into our new home quickly, and the kids were ecstatic about another sibling joining our brood. A new homeschool year was beginning, and I had a lot to do to prepare. But this pregnancy was pretty rough at the beginning. I had horrible nausea the first four months, and it wasn't just morning sickness, it was all day every day sickness. There were many days when I would line up three chairs by the big bay window that looked into the backyard and hand the kids binoculars and bird books. They would spend hours looking for different types of birds and document all of them in their science notebook. Thankfully our backyard was a haven for birds, and by the time I finally started feeling better the kids had identified over fifty species.

The remainder of my pregnancy went smoothly and on February 11th at 7:27 am, our fourth miracle baby, Noah Jonathan Stone, was born. He was incredibly perfect in every way. We were blessed beyond belief.

Noah's first year was completely normal. Joshua and Jacob gladly shared a room, so that Noah could have a room of his own. Life with four children was chaotically amazing, and we loved it. Noah began his second year full of life and joy and then when he was fifteen months old Noah stopped being Noah. He stopped talking, smiling and making eye contact. He spent hours banging his head on the floor and in his crib. He cried all night long every night. He would sit for hours during the day in a daze not reacting to anything or anyone around him. We stopped going out to eat because Noah would panic and flee under the table. He would be inconsolable until we would just give up and leave. I went months without a full night's sleep, because I would have to sit in the rocking chair with him all night trying to comfort him.

After months of pursuing medical help we were finally given a diagnosis that broke our hearts; our son had autism. We grieved for our son and wondered what the future would hold for him and for us. Family and friends rallied around us, and with their support we began our life with a new normal.

I spent a majority of the next few years researching and learning all I could about autism and spent almost every waking moment doing everything possible to keep our son connected to our world. Through it all I was sure of one thing; God was in control. He had provided this miracle baby to us, and He trusted us to provide Noah with everything he needed to be successful and happy in life. With assistance from our local school district we enrolled Noah into a Preschool Program for Children with Disabilities program (PPCD). The teachers gave an amazing amount of support to Noah in and out of school. The school district provided us an occupational therapist, speech therapist and an in-home support person that allowed us to maximize each day for Noah in our efforts to make him successful.

And Noah responded. There were many days that he wanted to shut down and turn inward blocking the world out, but he fought to stay connected to us. Noah knew he wasn't in this alone. Our other children were intentional in including Noah into every aspect of their day. Family and friends overlooked the awkward moments and loved our son unconditionally. We joined together and committed ourselves to making Noah's world a place where he could fulfill the purpose and plan God had for his life.

And that is what we have done ever since. He is now a remarkable young man. He has worked hard to overcome the barriers that autism creates and has a heart as big as Texas. He loves unconditionally and is a daily example of the heart of the Father. Noah has the ability to see things in the spiritual realm that most of us will never see and he speaks truth with such maturity and depth that we stand amazed most days at the gift the Lord has deposited within him. I can't imagine life without him and our family is all the richer because of him. His future is held firmly in the loving hands of a God who has destined him to do great things, and we can't wait to see the kingdom impact our son will make.

God, your Word says that Your love for us is unconditional and unending. I choose to believe that no matter what my past might have been, or the imperfections or struggles I might deal with in my life, I will I choose to believe in and receive Your love. I will stand firmly rooted in the knowledge that Your love looks past every blemish and imperfection I might have. I will embrace that love so that I will know and experience just how wide, how long and how deep Your love truly is for me. I am not alone.

The God Who Sees Us

Psalm 33:13-15

From heaven the Lord looks down and sees all mankind; from His dwelling place He watches all who live on earth; He who forms the hearts of all, who considers everything they do.

CHAPTER 25

During those years I began teaching again and in 1997 I became the assistant to the Athletic Director at a private Christian school. In the summer of that year I received our varsity football schedule and immediately noticed a very unique opponent on the schedule. We were going to have the opportunity to play a team that came from a very unusual place; a maximum-security youth prison. These young men were in prison for some pretty serious crimes. They had to work really hard to earn the privilege of being a part of the football team.

I began to ask questions about the circumstances behind these young men and about how the team was formed. I learned that they came from all walks of life and that most of them had not experienced a loving or nurturing home. They had made some really poor choices along the way and were now paying the penalty for those choices. The boys earned the privilege of being a part of the team by meeting quite a lengthy list of standards set by the warden of the prison. They had no home field, so every game was an away game for them. Most of their parents were either not involved in their lives or were too far away to ever visit. The team had no home crowd, no cheerleaders and no one to support them. The amazing staff of the prison did its best to come to as many games as possible but there were only a handful that could attend on a weekly basis.

I thought about what a great ministry opportunity this presented our school, so I went to the Athletic Director (AD) and asked him if I could contact other schools and find out if they did anything to minister to the team when they had played them. Over the next four weeks I gathered information and then met with our AD again. I shared with him some ideas I had collected from the other schools but told him that no one had really organized a real ministry opportunity. I asked him that day if I could put into action a plan that incorporated some of those ideas and a few other ideas I had. I knew it would allow our school to minister the love of Jesus to those boys. He was all for it. With the game quickly approaching I reached out to some of my friends at the school that I knew would jump at the opportunity to minister to these young men. Our plans came together very quickly and our AD sent out an email to all our parents asking for their support. The email shared that this was a wonderful opportunity for all of us to come together to show the love of Jesus to these boys who were in desperate need of hearing the message of hope that only the Lord can bring.

Parents were asked to come dressed in the opponent's team colors and sit on the opponent's sideline to cheer for them. Our cheerleaders were divided into two groups and half of the girls became cheerleaders for the other team. Our elementary students created large signs for each of the players, parents gathered items together to create incredible gift bags for each of the boys. Our varsity boys each wrote a handwritten letter to the boys that were tucked inside a devotional Bible that we put in each gift bag. One of our parents made homemade cookies and decorated them with the numbers of each of the players. A dad grilled hamburgers onsite and prepared food and sides for the bus ride home. Netanya even got to help one of my friends create a huge breakthrough banner for the boys to run through.

The whole school was so excited for that game! Friday night finally came and we had arranged for a pre-game meal for the team in our cafeteria. They arrived at about five fifteen on a regular looking yellow school bus, but this was not your ordinary school bus. This bus had guards with guns that exited the bus, scanned the cafeteria and then brought the team in single file with guards at either end of the line. The boys feasted on some great barbeque and our AD shared an amazing message with them about life and hope. The team walked through their pre-game on the field and then was escorted to the locker room to rest for a few minutes before game time. They couldn't have dreamed what was about to happen to them.

As they warmed up a few more minutes in the end zone and began to walk around to the opponent sideline our AD started motioning to them to come toward him. They all held back, because what they saw was a sixty-yard spirit line on two sides with a huge breakthrough banner at the front. They assumed that the line was for our boys and tried to start walking the other way but our AD continued to motion them toward the back of the breakthrough. It wasn't until their coach came over and started telling them that the spirit line was for THEM that they actually understood what was happening. None of them had ever experienced a typical Friday night football game in Texas, but they were getting ready to for the very first time!

Those boys broke through the banner with all that was in them and as the spirit line began to scream and yell FOR the boys, those young men transformed right there in the middle of the field. They experienced a flood of love and support that began to bubble up and out of them, and it couldn't be held back. By the time they reached the end of the spirit line they were absolutely giddy, jumping up and down, high-fiving each other and slapping each other on the back. It looked like they were getting ready to play in the Super Bowl. As the spirit line broke up many of our families sat down in the bleachers on the opponent's side and began loudly cheering for the boys. When they would make a great tackle or catch a pass, the bleachers erupted with excitement. The boys were so confused they kept turning around looking at our parents in disbelief. They couldn't believe that someone was actually cheering FOR them, BY NAME. Within a few minutes the reality of what was happening finally hit the boys, and they began to play like never before. Their enthusiasm for each other and their joy was so much fun to watch.

The final score didn't matter to them. When the game clock hit 0:00 they grabbed their water bottles and circled around their coach to shower him with water like they had just WON the Super Bowl. The teams met at midfield and as we always did, players and fans circled up to pray. Our AD spoke for a few minutes and as he got ready to pray one of the boys from the other team asked if he could pray; and pray he did. That young man gave thanks to God, he gave thanks for the people gathered around them that didn't even know them, but had made them feel loved and special. He gave thanks for being able to experience such an amazing night, and he asked for God to bless all of us.

The boys climbed back aboard their bus with hearts full of love and hope. We were told a few weeks later that there had been an unbelievable change at the prison. The boys' attitudes had totally transformed. They were respectful, attentive and eager to help. They were becoming leaders within the prison walls. One of our parents provided a DVD of the game for them and they watched it almost every night reliving the moment in time that strangers showed compassion and love to them. It was a night none of us will ever forget. Once again God showed all of us that we don't walk this life alone. Even when we make poor choices, there is always forgiveness, redemption and restoration. He sees past our mistakes and sees the child He created us to be, and He loves us through it all.

—∞—

God, your Word says that you look down from heaven and see us. I choose to acknowledge the mistakes I have made and seek forgiveness from those I have hurt. I will look for ways to bring Your love, Your joy and Your hope to others who need to know You. I will not forget all You have done for me, and how Your love has brought new life to me. I am not alone.

The God Who Deserves Our Praise

Revelation 4:11

You are worthy, our Lord and God, to receive glory and honor and power, for You created all things, and by Your will they were created and have their being.

CHAPTER 26

It took almost nineteen years for full reconciliation and restoration to occur between my dad and his children. In 2010, Daddy gave his life to the Lord and the healing that began with that decision was remarkable. His new relationship with us brought new revelation and understanding. Daddy battled several forms of cancer over the last several years of his life and in the summer of 2012 he was given just a few weeks to live. My brother, sister and I were able to spend the last week of his life by his bedside. I finally felt the love of my father that I had sought for so many years in my youth. That week was a time of emotional healing for all of us. At 8:00 a.m. on August 22, 2012, Daddy walked into the loving arms of his Savior. I was so privileged to be able to hold his hand as he slipped out of his cancer-ridden body to begin eternity with a new and perfect body. I am honored to have been his daughter and to have had the privilege of calling him Daddy.

At the time of publication, my son Joshua is now married. He and his wife Tabitha live in a neighboring town and we love having them so close. He has grown into a man who appreciates life, who loves deeply and values family above all else. He and his wife are actively involved in their church, and Joshua is part of the worship team. He overcame several obstacles and graduated from college with a degree in Management Information Systems. He works in the IT world and is our go to guy for all things technology. He and Tabitha have blessed us with our first grandchild, Ava Marie. She brings unspeakable joy to my heart. Their second daughter Emma will arrive very soon.

Jacob is married to Skyler, his best friend since fifth grade, and they live in the same town we do. They are a powerhouse couple and are an incredible example of the success that comes from hard work, integrity and perseverance. He obtained his college degree in Business Administration and his Masters of Business degree in just under five years. They are members of the same church we attend, and we love being able to worship together. Jacob works for the Dallas Cowboys and is a very successful businessman. He lives out his Christian faith with no reservations and is well regarded in the marketplace.

Noah is a junior in high school now and continues to amaze us. He maintains an A/B average, has played select basketball, works at a local restaurant and is now a licensed driver. His spiritual maturity grows deeper each year, and he shares so many profound truths with us that I now keep a journal to write everything down that the Lord shows him.

And what about our beautiful rainbow? She has entered a new season of life as she begins her second year of college at Texas A&M University. She is an incredibly gifted artist, an amazing chef and an excellent student who finished her first year of college with a 3.80 average. Her tenacity for life is insatiable, and she fills every minute of our days with laughter and love. Her love for children has led her to many different opportunities over the last several years including being a nanny, working in her school's after school day care and teaching two and three year olds in our church's children's ministry. She is pursuing a degree in Communications and is very involved in a Christian artist group at A&M.

God has grown me in ways I never imagined possible. Today I am confident in the knowledge that He sees me and delights in using my gifts and talents in so many different ways. I know now that my voice matters and that He is able to speak love, wisdom, strength, encouragement and confidence through me to my family, friends, co-workers and all those He brings to my path. I love to share my story with others; the story of how this lonely, broken little girl has been redeemed and set free from the lies that once penetrated my heart and mind so deeply and completely. His love has allowed me to find resounding joy in each day and peace in every circumstance.

Todd and I will celebrate thirty-one years of marriage this year, and we love each other more deeply with each passing year. He is still my hero and my best friend. The sweetest blessing that Todd and I have been given by our children is that all of them have given their hearts and their lives to the One who gave THEM life. They walk daily hand in hand with the Lord, they trust Him for each step they take and they allow His Holy Spirit to guide them through this wonderful thing called life. They know that with God they will never be alone. They understand that His eye is always on them and His hand of provision will always rest on them. A parent can find no greater joy, and we are forever grateful to a loving God who created each of them and then tenderly placed them into our waiting arms. This one thing I know and of this one thing I am sure; He is a God who is faithful, true and His character is unchanging. His love for us never wavers, never falters and is never ending. He will never leave us alone, and He is worthy of all our praise.

God, your Word says You brought creation into being. Everything I enjoy, everything I have is because of Your great love for me. I choose to praise You. I will daily remember to thank You for all the blessings in my life and when trials come, I will praise You because I know You are always with me. I am not alone.

The God Who Calls Us His Own

Ephesians 3:16-19

God decided in advance to adopt us into His own family by bringing us to Himself through Jesus Christ. This is what He wanted to do, and it gave Him great pleasure. So we praise God for the glorious grace He has poured out on us who belong to His dear Son.

CHAPTER 27

As I began writing this book my initial intention was simply to tell our adoption story. My desire was to take the words from a journal I kept during the process of adopting Netanya and turn them into a book that I could share with her. I wanted her to always be able to look back and see how much she is loved. I wanted her to know that the baby that had been abandoned and left alone on a cold dark step was no longer an orphan and that she would never be alone again. She had a forever family and a home to call her own. And more importantly, she had a loving God who had watched over her from the moment He created her.

But as the words began to fill the pages, God began to reveal His purpose. As I have shared throughout this book, there have been experiences in my life that left me feeling alone and unseen. Our journey to our daughter was not an easy one, and there were many times over those long months that my husband and I were brought to our knees. Yet each time our knees buckled, each time we felt alone, God revealed Himself to us in a new and creative way. He gave us the strength to stand and believe again. He showed us so many facets of His true character during that season, and now we have a much deeper understanding of who God truly is in our lives and just how much He loves us.He wants you to know Him like that too. He wants you to see how much He loves you.

**Have you ever felt like an orphan?
Do you feel abandoned or alone?**

Has life overwhelmed you? Is there a situation that has caused you to lose hope? If your answer is yes, God would love to step in and allow you to experience the same truth I have learned through my life experiences.

You are never alone.

He wants you to fully grasp the knowledge that no matter what trial you may be facing, no matter what hurt you may have experienced and no matter what has happened in your past or in your present, He loves you and He is there for you. He longs to call you His own. He wants to speak life, love, joy, peace and hope into your life.

Just as we relentlessly pursued our daughter, God is relentless in His pursuit of you. He looks past what you have done and how you have acted and instead sees all that you can be. He sees the purpose and plan He created you to fulfill. He sees the amazing difference you will make in this world. And He wants you to see all that too. His greatest desire is for you to be part of His family.

There is one thing YOU need to do. You have to let Him in.

Romans 3:23 states, "all have sinned and fallen short of the glory of God." We mess up, we sin and the Bible tells us that the consequence of sin is death. Romans 6:23 states, "For the price of sin is death, but the free gift of God is eternal life through Christ."

Our sin won't allow us to experience eternal life with God, but Romans 5:8 has good news for us, "God showed His great love for us by sending Christ to die for us while we were still sinners." There is that relentless pursuit I was talking about. That is how much God loves us. He so wants us to experience the joy of being a part of His family that He sent His only Son to die for us, for **you** and for **me**. Jesus willingly paid the price for our mess, our sin. He went to the cross and died, so we could experience freedom here on earth and for eternity. He came to save us from eternal death.

So what do we need to do? How do we let Him in?

We have to acknowledge that we have sinned; we need Him in our lives, and then invite Him in. Romans 10:9,13 says,

> If you confess with your mouth that Jesus is Lord and believe in your heart that God raised Him from the dead, you will be saved. For it is by believing in your heart that you are made right with God, and it is by confessing with your mouth that you are saved. "For everyone who calls on the name of the LORD will be saved."

It's really that simple, open your heart and by faith, acknowledge that Jesus took your sin to the cross and paid the price for you, and you will be saved. Your life will be forever changed. Your decision to give Him permission to lead and guide you through His Holy Spirit will be the best decision you ever make because you are now part of HIS family. From that moment on you will never be alone. Romans 5:1 says,

> Therefore, since we have been made right in God's sight by faith, we have peace with God because of what Jesus Christ has done for us.

As His child you will experience an unconditional, unending love from a Father that will remain by your side through every peak and valley of life. You will find peace in the middle of the storm. You will find strength you never knew you had. You will have hope in the midst of darkness and a joy that will resonate up from the deepest part of your being.

As you continue to trust Him with each day that lies before you and spend time in His Word, you will truly begin to understand the true character of God. As you allow His Holy Spirit to become a part of your everyday life He will show you the areas where healing, repentance or forgiveness need to happen. He will bring trustworthy people to you, pastors, small group leaders and Christian friends, who through prayer and counsel will help you walk through those areas. And as you receive healing in those broken places you will experience even more freedom, more joy and more peace. Your life will never be the same because no matter where you are or what you are walking through you will have the assurance that God is right there with you.

Just as I stood on steps of that police station so many years ago and whispered to my baby girl that she would never be abandoned again, God wants to tell you the same thing. And just like I told her God had created her in His image, and He was proud of who she is God wants you to know He is proud of you too.

He loves you. He is here for you. He has great plans for you. It is the message of hope He longs to give each of us, because that is who He is. And you, as His child are His most cherished possession.

***You* are no longer an orphan.**

***You* are not alone.**

Joshua at three months

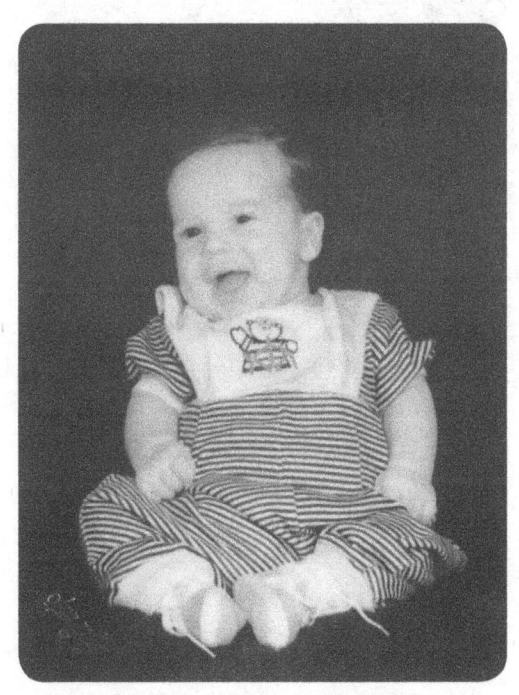

Jacob at three months

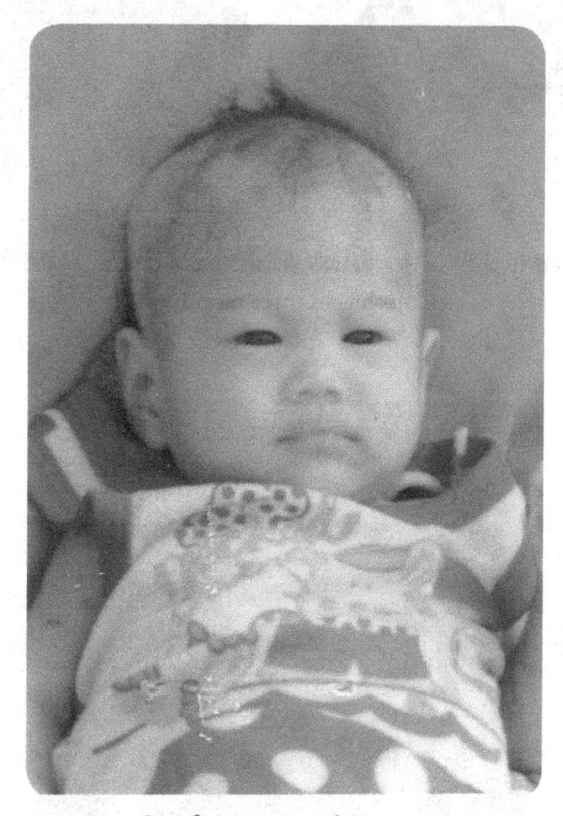

Our first picture of Netanya

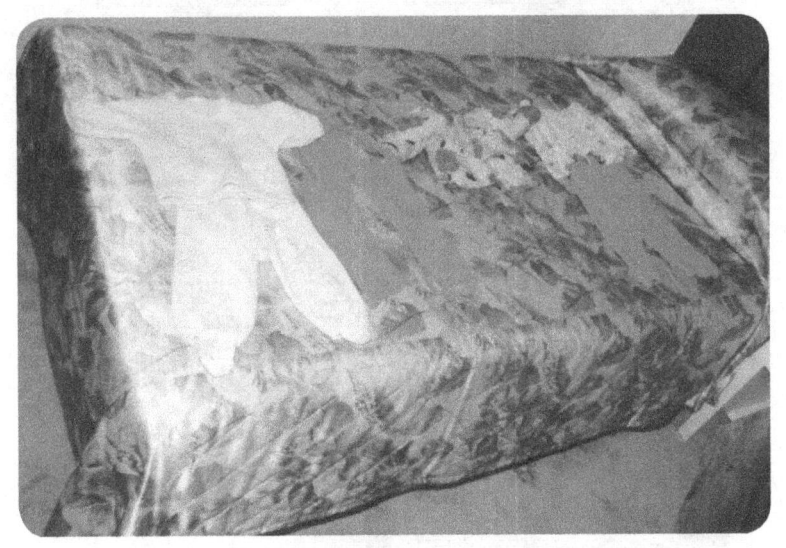

Some of the layers of clothing Netanya wore

Singing her song to her for the first time

At the Police station in Changsha

Mr. Samuel Lamb and Netanya

Home at last!

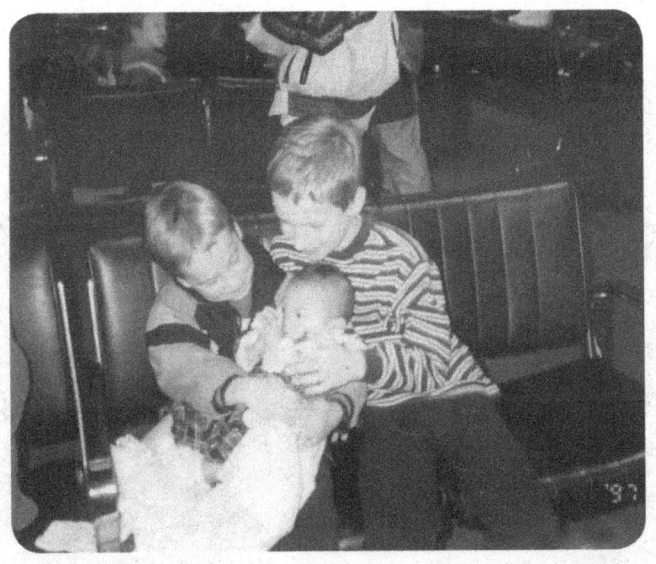

Joshua and Jacob meeting their sister for the first time

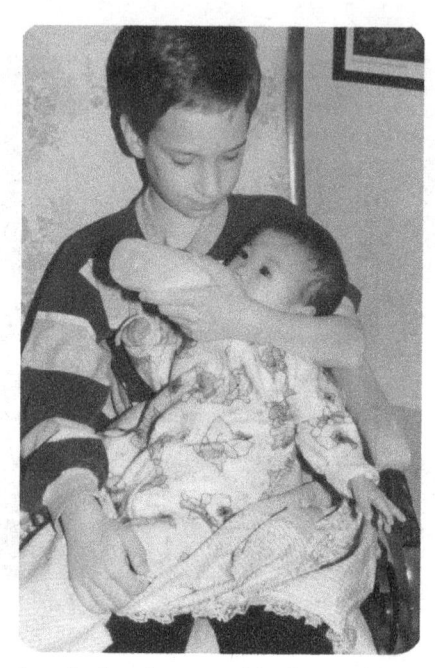

Joshua feeding his sister her first night home

Introducing Netanya to our church family

Proud big brothers

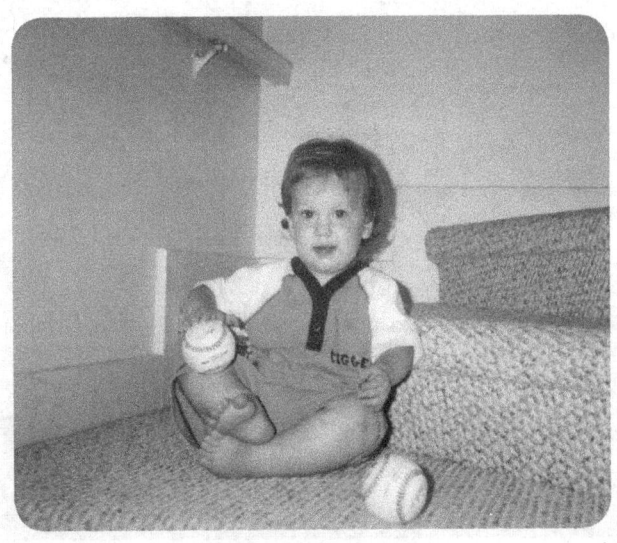

Noah at four months

Netanya 2015

Our family 2015

CPSIA information can be obtained
at www.ICGtesting.com
Printed in the USA
LVHW100048060122
707977LV00025B/663

9 781512 705416